It is with great happiness
that I share with you
the beautiful story of
my brother's life.

Ann Burke

The Bishop Who Dared

A BIOGRAPHY OF
BISHOP MICHAEL RYAN DEMPSEY

"Let all Christians stand in the first
rank of those who DARE by every
means at their disposal to break the
hellish circle of poverty."
— *POPE PAUL VI*

by Ann Dempsey Burke

Valkyrie Press, Inc.

First Edition
International Standard Book No. 0-912760-72-9
Library of Congress Catalog Card No. 78-55556

Published by

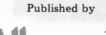

Valkyrie
Press,Inc.

2135-2149 1st Avenue South
St. Petersburg, Florida 33712

To Our Parents

and

All Those Who Loved Him

ACKNOWLEDGMENTS

I wish to express my sincere appreciation to all the people who have helped me to tell the beautiful story of my brother's life. I am especially grateful to the late Reverend Philip Cahill, to Mr. and Mrs. Robert Squires, Mr. James Prior, Dr. Robert Botthof, the Staff of the Campaign For Human Development, and the people who worked in the Inner-City of Chicago with Bishop Dempsey.

The Right Reverend Michael Ryan Dempsey, D.D., Auxiliary Bishop of Chicago.

FOREWORD

Michael Ryan Dempsey was a great man. As his sister, I knew him for a lifetime, and I would like to share my own treasured memories of him enhanced by the memories of countless others whose lives he touched.

I watched him grow from the small boy who was my constant companion to a man of authority who shouldered almost incredible responsibilities.

Mike could have been successful in almost any field of endeavor. He chose a life of service — a life for which he was uniquely qualified. He chose the poor for his friends, and he considered it his personal privilege and responsibility to work with them and for them. His simple background prepared him to fit so well into their lifestyle.

In this biography I have attempted to reconstruct his life through each of its many phases. He was, in turn, a student, a priest, a teacher, a pastor, and a bishop, and simultaneously, an unflinching advocate for the poor.

During his thirty years in the priesthood Mike deviated in many ways from the common path. As a parish priest he could have been content performing the many duties ordinarily associated with parish work, and he would have well earned the respect of the people he served. But he thought he should do more. He believed the Church should be active in employment and housing and in whatever areas the needs of the people indicated.

As a bishop, he could have limited his activities to administrative tasks. But he made a conscious choice to continue as a parish priest while using the office of bishop in the most positive way, in what he considered to be the true spirit of the Church — to help the poor. So, when the Church proposed the Campaign for Human Development, the role of national director seemed to have been designed for him, and he moved into a much larger sphere of service.

I think that Mike's idea of what the modern Church should be to the people stemmed from his literal interpretation of the spirit of the early Church — the spirit that was carried to the world by the people who had recently seen and heard Christ, and who were overflowing with love for their fellowmen and fired with the faith that could move mountains.

Though Mike was anachronistic even in his early years in the priesthood, after Vatican II, when Pope John XXIII called for the updating of the Church, Mike stood in the forefront of where he thought the Church should be in the 1960s, not only in terms of social change, but also in liturgical change. He saw liturgical change as a means of stimulating the members of the Church and as a device for attracting others.

Father Peter Powell, an Episcopal priest, said of him: "It was Bishop Dempsey who taught me, by his own episcopate, that a bishop's deepest commitment must be to being a servant, rather than a Prince of the Church. No bishop of our time set a greater example of holiness than did Bishop Dempsey. He was all Our Lord wanted His apostles to be: loving, warm, sensitive, generous, devout, infinitely humble, but everlastingly strong.

"He was a quiet but moving speaker. However, eloquent as his words were, his actions were much more eloquent. He was a man of exceptional vision; but he was equally a man who knew how to deal with realities. First and foremost he was God's priest. Thus, his life centered upon his pleading of the Holy Sacrifice of the Altar. Then, filled with the life and power of Christ in the Holy Eucharist, he carried the God-Man into the lives of everyone with whom he came in contact. An exemplary, self-sacrificing priest in his own life, he nevertheless was one of the greatest fund-raisers I have ever known. He begged wondrously because he never begged for himself. He spoke to me, and to many another priest, of how we must see the Son of God present in His poor. He said the same thing to City Hall; and City Hall responded in terms that benefitted God's poor: new housing, increased jobs, Federal and Municipal grants so great in size that the amounts amaze me to this day. People were so deeply moved by Bishop Dempsey's own love of God and His poor that they became generous beyond any bounds of generosity to which they had committed themselves before. For the bishop possessed a wonderful combination of holiness and practicality. We priests who were privileged to know him, found our own vocations renewed and transformed each time we were in Bishop Dempsey's presence. In him we saw fulfilled in reality what most priests can only dream of being."

The Bishop Who Dared

A BIOGRAPHY OF BISHOP MICHAEL RYAN DEMPSEY

TABLE OF CONTENTS

CHAPTER ONE

BRANCHES OF THE FAMILY TREE

HE WAS THERE every day. There could be no more exciting place in the world for my brother than the Westside of Chicago. And his community was like all other poor communities in the world. Mike Dempsey didn't study the poor and write about them from a comfortable desk in a university; he loved the poor and lived with them in the ghettos of our big city.

In telling the story of Mike's life, I would like first to introduce our parents and grandparents, because it was through them and the generations that preceded them that Mike received his opportunity to live and to share in our great heritage of faith.

Both of our parents, Edward Aloysious Dempsey and Mary Ryan Dempsey, were born in Chicago in 1889, in the vicinity of Ashland and North Avenues; but they did not meet until much later, after both families had moved to Logan Square in the northwest section of the city.

Mother and Dad were married on July 26, 1917. They chose this day because it was the feast of St. Ann as well as Dad's twenty-eighth birthday. World War I was still going on, and the possibility of Dad's being drafted into service hung heavily over them. However, the Armistice came the following year, and Dad was never called.

Dad was a photoengraver by trade. After completing his four-year apprenticeship, he entered the newspaper field with the old *Record-Herald.*

Probably because his father and his two brothers were firemen, Dad had a real attachment to the Fire Department, and through the years he frequently visited his friends at Engine Company 106. There he would enjoy monitoring the "ticker-tape" calls or reminiscing about the big five-elevens.

In appearance, Dad was of medium height, with dark, curly hair and prominent dark eyebrows. During the course of time he added many, many pounds to the boyish figure he had when he married Mother. As was characteristic of the Dempsey family, Dad's hair turned gray prematurely. He would laughingly say, "Your mother does the worrying and I get the gray hair."

Mother was a gentle, petite lady, with deep blue eyes and neatly-rolled dark hair that formed a soft frame for her face. She was a very gracious person. Her innate seriousness contrasted with Dad's sense of humor. Her ability to feel deeply the happiness or the sadness of others might have been attributed to her Irish nature.

Mother's only career was that of homemaker, but her talent with paints provided her with a pleasant hobby. In her younger years she had read much poetry, and it always amazed us that she could quote the poets whenever the occasion arose.

Jim Dempsey, Dad's father, was born in Chicago too. Possibly seeing the Chicago Fire in 1871 had inspired him to become a fireman. At the time of his death he was the oldest member of the department. Grandfather had the dubious honor of being related to Mrs. O'Leary, whose cow, the history books said, kicked over a lantern and thus started the "big fire" which caused the new city of Chicago to burn.

Grandmother Ellen Mylett Dempsey came from County Roscommon in Ireland. It had been her loving concern for the safety of her fireman-husband which prompted her to listen constantly for the sound of the horse-drawn engines in the early days. Her children naturally grew up with a great awareness of the fire sirens.

Grandmother lived a long life and always retained her charming brogue. Even in her old age she was the essence of patience with children.

Our maternal grandfather, Michael Ryan, was born in Tipperary. Having had only a third-grade education in Ireland, he studied endlessly. His family greatly respected him for being a self-educated man. Mother said that, when her brother Jim attended law school at the University of Notre Dame, he sent his dissertations home to be corrected by his father.

Grandfather Ryan was a born poet; he became a successful plumbing contractor, in addition to serving seven terms as an alderman. He died when our mother was only fourteen years old.

Not only was my brother the recipient of our grandfather's name, but he inherited a short, slight build, a brilliant mind, and a propensity for politics. However, the latter trait did not become apparent until Mike Dempsey, in extending his wholehearted efforts to the cause of the poor, found himself dealing not only with the hierarchy of the Church, but with the Mayor, the vice president, and the government officials who headed the poverty programs.

Then, there was Grandmother Ann Feeney Ryan. She too had come from Tipperary. She married Grandfather in the final days of the Civil War, and for a while they lived at the Union Army base in Kentucky where he had been assigned. She lived through the hard times and the good. It must have been only a strong faith in God that sustained the Ryans in the days of the black diphtheria plague that claimed the lives of several of their small children. Our mother was the thirteenth and youngest of the family.

I remember Grandmother living on Logan Boulevard in a stone house that resembled an Irish castle. Back in the days when cows grazed in front of the Ryan home, their street was called Humboldt Boulevard, because it branched off from the boulevard which extended north from beautiful Humboldt Park. As the community grew, and the roads were paved, Grandmother, being the alderman's wife, was given the honor of renaming the boulevard. She chose the name "Logan" because she felt that John A. Logan, the illustrious senator from Illinois, should be remembered.

Grandfather Dempsey gave this account of the first Dempsey-Ryan meeting. Jim Dempsey was a young man when he went to City Hall to apply for a job in the Fire Department. When he walked into the office of Mayor Carter Harrison, the Mayor was not in, and Alderman Mike Ryan was at the desk. After accepting Jim's application, the alderman reached into the Mayor's desk drawer and offered Jim a cigar. Jim was surprised and said, "You mean you're giving me the Mayor's cigar?"

"Don't worry about it," Mike answered. "I know whom I'm giving it to."

He could hardly have foreseen the future, when his own daughter and the prospective fireman's son, who were yet to be born, would marry and produce the bishop who was to bear the combination of their names.

CHAPTER TWO

EARLY DAYS IN LOGAN SQUARE

"It was a great day for the Irish—
The day our Mike was born.
The Dempseys and the Ryans launched
A holiday that morn."

ALTHOUGH THESE WORDS were written about him many years later, they did apply that September 10, in 1918, when Michael Ryan Dempsey arrived in Chicago's Westside Hospital.

He was the first child born to our parents and was welcomed with great joy.

Mother's sister and brother, Dais and John Ryan, were the godparents who spoke for their little nephew and promised his faithfulness to God, as he was officially received into the Church which he was to serve so well. Aunt Dais, whose real name was Sarah, had presented him with a long white baptismal dress which he wore to St. Sylvester's Church that warm Sunday afternoon in September. She had included much love in the making of it.

While Michael was still an infant, Mother and Dad took him to visit their friend Katie O'Malley. Katie was a very holy woman, and she was blind. While she was holding the new baby she said, "It comes to me that this little boy will grow up to be a priest."

I don't know if Katie was prophetic, but her words did become a reality.

It was almost two years later when I came into the family. Michael and I soon began to develop a close friendship. Having my confident, amiable brother at my side was a real source of strength to me which never diminished with the years.

Our sister Agnes was born on Washington's Birthday in 1924. This was her special claim to fame, with the prospect of a school holiday every birthday. She was named Agnes Loretta to honor two of Dad's sisters.

Michael entered Brentano School that September. The friendly principal was in his office on orientation day to greet all the new students who were waiting in a long line to register for the new term. He extended his hand to my brother and said, "My name is Mr. Chase. What is yours?" Imagine Mother's embarrassment when her little darling replied, "Who chases you?"

Our first-grader's hair was dark and very curly, and locks

16

drooped over his forehead. His big brown eyes contained a spark of mischief, and he was already radiating the smile that was to characterize him the rest of his life.

Attending school was a happy experience for Michael because he was most eager to learn; but his days in that particular classroom were numbered. When winter came, his asthma, which had at times flared up in the past, became so severe that he had to drop out of school. Probably this was Mike's first real disappointment, and it was a difficult one for a six-year-old to bear. Fortunately, with good care, the asthma subsided and he was anxiously looking forward to the next fall when he would begin school again.

By that time we had moved a few blocks away, into a newly-built apartment building at 2902 North Francisco Avenue. Michael went into first grade at St. Francis Xavier's School. I followed a year later.

St. Francis was a German community although it was adjacent to the Irish parish, St. Sylvester's. Many parishes were ethnic. It seemed that the early immigrants had preferred to live among their own. Priests assigned to ethnic parishes usually knew the language of their people.

Right from the start, Mike was the kind of fellow who liked to spend as much time as possible at school. He left home early in the morning so that he could clean erasers, or empty wastebaskets for his teacher; or he would play "king of the hill" in the sand piles that were the makings of the new St. Francis' Church.

Often on the way to school he enjoyed walking alongside the "clooping" horse that pulled the milkman's wagon. Little Mike marvelled at the horse's knowing where to stop for the next delivery.

The school yard was a pleasant place, especially for the very young children. The Sisters of St. Francis who taught us would spend most of their lunch hour outside playing games with the children, so that there was a very friendly relationship between the teachers and the students. It was by coincidence that Mike had the name of the World Heavyweight Boxing Champion, Jack Dempsey, who was very prominent at this time. Because his name suggested strength, Mike was in demand when the boys in the school yard were choosing sides for games.

The two priests who resided at St. Francis were the only priests my brother knew; and I'm sure that they both made a great impression upon him at this early age. Father Martin Weidner was a young priest. He would frequently walk around outside of the school and talk to every child he met. He was the one who instructed the children for First Communion. Occasionally Father Weidner would visit at our home, and he would bring us a bag of penny candies which we children thought were more delicious because they came from him.

Our pastor was Father Edward Goldsmith. He was Jewish and a convert to the Church. I can remember Father Goldsmith sitting on a long, low radiator at the end of the first floor corridor in the school. As the children walked out in orderly fashion, the elderly priest would reach out for one of them and hold this little boy or girl on his lap. He was the picture of a loving pastor.

Mike and I usually were late returning from school because we couldn't resist walking a few times around the foundation of a new apartment building. Balancing on the narrow cement framework and then jumping over the spaces for doors and windows was a delightful sport. This was during the pre-Depression building boom and large apartment houses were being erected on many of the vacant "baseball" lots in our neighborhood.

At home Michael built an altar which conveniently fit into a corner of our dining room. He was then about eight years old. Having an altar was his own idea, but he needed some help from Dad in covering an orange crate and a cigar box with heavy white paper generously provided by our butcher. Thus the boxes were transformed into an altar and a tabernacle. Mom used her water colors to tint the white altar with shades of gold, and she painted a chalice on the tabernacle. Then tiny, colorful flowers in slender vases were added. Aunt Dais shopped around downtown and located minute candle-holders for the clusters of birthday candles which were placed on either side of the altar. Mike found some lace curtains that Mother wasn't using. When he draped them around his shoulders, they became his vestments. It was at this altar that he attempted to repeat Father Weidner's sermons.

Dad would laugh later when he told about the time that Mike had done something mischievous. As Dad was running after him, little Mike stopped to genuflect at the altar. Dad just couldn't scold him then, and he decided to drop the charges.

In another corner of our dining room, our first radio was a small crystal set with earphones, set up on a card table. Charles Lindbergh was making the first solo flight across the Atlantic

Ocean. Though excessive static made reception of the news a little difficult, it was nonetheless exciting. Like all the boys, Mike had a wooden "Lindy" airplane. Agnes' doll was the passenger riding recklessly in his plane.

After my brother finished third grade, we moved again, just a short distance and still within the Logan Square area. We transferred to Brentano School that September.

Brentano was an excellent school both academically and from the standpoint of discipline. The teachers, as I remember them, were mostly single or widowed, and they were totally dedicated to their students. They, in turn, expected complete cooperation from the students, and they had no qualms about punishing misbehavior. Some teachers proudly remembered distinguished Brentano graduates such as Notre Dame's coach, Knute Rockne, and Hollywood's Ralph Bellamy.

There was quite a Christian atmosphere in this public school. At the beginning of each day the loud singing of hymns could be heard coming from all of the classrooms. Many teachers knew the religious affiliations of all their students and encouraged everyone to go to church.

Although the teachers were not allowed to teach religion *per se*, they could stress moral principles, and they did. It might well have been in Brentano that Mike learned his first lessons in ecumenism.

He and I, upon entering public school, were immediately enrolled in religious instruction classes at St. John Berchman's, which was now our parish church. We were taught by priests. Mother always made a conscientious effort to help us memorize our catechism very well. She instilled in us the importance of making our service to God the chief concern of our lives.

Our parents still referred to St. John's as the Belgian church, although there were few Belgians left, and, as in most neighborhoods, a mixture of nationalities had come in. But the Belgian Hall at Fullerton and Rockwell brought the old-timers back, especially for the annual Memorial Day observance. On that morning, a parade began at the Belgian Hall, and paraders, dressed in native costumes, marched through the streets in step with a loudly-playing band. They proceeded to St. John's for Mass; and a day of festivities followed.

The Irish weren't sending their children to public schools in those years because the Church was adamant in stressing Catholic education. But Mother had a sentimental attachment to Brentano, since it was her alma mater, and she was convinced that public sch ,ols provided a fine education and that we could find only good companions among such young children. Our parents thought that religious training at home was most essential. However, they strongly felt that, on the high school level, we should have the influence of the Sisters and priests.

Teachers really appreciated Michael Dempsey. He was polite, cooperative, and possessed of a real enthusiasm for learning. His ability to put his whole heart into the things that he considered important was already noticeable at this young age.

On the first day of May, in 1929, we welcomed our sister Kathryn into the family. Kathryn was quite the family "pet"; and, as time went on, Mike, Agnes, and I delighted in taking her out for walks to acquaint her with the outside world of our neighborhood. She was Mike's protegé. By the time Kathryn was three years old, Mike had taught her to identify pictures of people and places in his United States history book. Hearing a child of that age pronounce names like Ulysses S. Grant brought us much laughter. Kathryn later shortened her name to Kay.

Throughout his Brentano days, Mike definitely showed that he had within him a great spirit of adventure, a necessary ingredient in the driving force which later spurred him on to accept many challenging tasks. The books that he read were always boys' stories of mystery and adventure. The movies that he sought out were the exciting African jungle expeditions of the Frank Buck "Bring-Em-Back-Alive" series.

But I had the opportunity to take part in his real life adventures in the big city in which we lived. Usually my geography wasn't the best, but Mike could find his way anywhere in Chicago, and I had every confidence in him. We were roamers. The city was much safer in those days, so that with only a few rules from home to observe, we were free to travel anywhere. We could ride a street car for three cents or a bus for a nickel. To ride on the open upper deck of a bus on a hot summer's day was a glorious experience. There were endless places to discover. Educational buildings such as the Museum of Science and Industry, the Field Museum, and the Historical Society were among Mike's favorites.

A day at Navy Pier was always enjoyable too. The street car would swing and sway to the far end of the pier, where there was a peninsula of carnival rides, food, and loud music. The music was muffled by the sound of the sweeping waves from Lake Michigan as they dashed against the pier. From the deck-like floor above this, we would watch the ships coming into dock as they curved their way from the Chicago River.

Often we would delight in just exploring a new neighborhood, where there would be new schools to see, open churches to visit, and friendly dogs to greet us.

Summers in Chicago were hot and sunny and beautiful, and we wished that they could last forever. But inevitably they would end, and Mike would be happy to rejoin his pals, Milton Zimmerman and Marshall Aeder, in school again. Possibly these boys were as much attracted to each other by their manifest good manners as they were by their common keen interest in learning; and unwittingly they competed for the highest marks in the classroom.

During these years, Mike had many bouts with asthma which sometimes caused him to miss several days of school. He would always bounce back again and quickly catch up with his class work. Mom was inclined to be very solicitous about his health, but Dad reminded her that to be overly protective would not be doing Mike a favor. So Mike was a patrol boy, rain or shine.

It was customary at Brentano for capable students to be advanced beyond their classmates, and in this way Michael regained the year he had lost in first grade. Mother was very happy about this accomplishment.

Early in eighth grade Mike was asked to speak at the school assembly on the day before Halloween. He was to compose his own speech, the purpose being to caution the children against Halloween pranks that would cause aggravation to others. Mike was the smallest boy in the eighth-grade class, but, when he walked out on the stage, he couldn't have looked bigger in the eyes of Agnes and me. Actually, this was his first sermon, and I still remember his opening words: "As we all know, tomorrow is Halloween. What we shall do tomorrow, most of us have already figured out." Then he went on to mention the usual mischief of dumping garbage cans and writing with soap on store windows. Probably Mike was chosen to speak because he obviously was not a prankster himself. He suggested that everyone participate in the planned activities in the parks and playgrounds. He knew from his own experience that they would have a good time.

My brother thoroughly enjoyed his last year at Brentano. History had always been his favorite subject. Now he found the study of civics equally interesting. He read everything in the newspapers that would inform him about what was going on in our government in Washington.

Long before graduation Mike had been expressing his desire to study for the priesthood. I think that ever since the days when we children set up a cardboard village on our living room floor, and with our gift of imagination operated the town of "Dempseyville," we girls naturally assumed that he would go on to the priesthood. This was because the only role he played in our game was that of parish priest.

It was rather unusual for a public schoolboy to enter a seminary, but his Brentano teachers were delighted, and they gave him much encouragement.

However, the fact that Mike had attended public school created a problem for him. Every prospective seminarian was required to bring a letter of recommendation from his pastor. Our pastor, Father Laurence Hurkmans, who was a fine-looking old Belgian fellow, said, "I can't recommend you because you didn't attend the parish school. I don't know you." Michael went home disheartened.

He returned another day, this time bringing his report cards; but Father Hurkmans put him off again.

On Mike's next visit the pastor commented, "You're a persistent fellow, aren't you?" But he still hadn't written a letter. Eventually, and possibly just to get rid of the boy, the priest produced a letter. Mike had already been in the school for some time.

Perhaps it was because of this experience that Mike, in his own priesthood, never made any distinction between the parochial and public school students.

CHAPTER THREE

THE GREAT DEPRESSION STRIKES US

SINCE MY BROTHER wished to become a Chicago diocesan priest, the school he would attend was Quigley Preparatory Seminary, at Chestnut and Rush Streets, near the old Water Tower.

About the time that he was graduating from grade school, in June of 1932, the recession which the whole country was experiencing was affecting us. For many years Dad had been employed by Barnes-Crosby, a privately-owned advertising company. Now, with the recession, the company was cutting down on expenditures, and Dad was no longer working a full week.

Our Model-T Ford, which was our only luxury, was the first comfort that we had to relinquish; and Dad never owned a car again. The little black Ford, which our father fondly called his "Tin Lizzie," had long been our means of transportation for our family outings. It was used for our weekly trips to Rogers Park, where Dad's parents had lived since Grandfather's retirement from the Fire Department. On Sundays our grandparents' home overflowed with people, and we children thoroughly enjoyed this day with our cousins, the Botthos, the Dempseys, the Houses, and the Tankers.

Like families all over the nation, we were to be greatly affected by the Depression. Looking back now, I am positive that we did benefit in many ways from the hardships that we had to endure. I believe that God, in His providence, was preparing Michael for his future work.

Shortly before my brother was to register for school, Barnes-Crosby had to close its doors, and Dad lost his job. The forthcoming expense of tuition was indeed of great concern to our parents. Mother accompanied Mike to Quigley on the day for registration so that she could explain our financial situation to the registrar. Both she and Mike were overjoyed when they learned that Mike would be most welcome to attend Quigley without paying tuition; and that he was offered a job in the school cafeteria to compensate for this gratuity.

So, when September came, Michael Dempsey entered the minor seminary where he was to spend five years that were to be very important in the shaping of the course of his life, and in the acquiring of new and priceless friendships.

One of these friendships began on the first day of school when Mike met Alfred Abramowicz. The two were to be consecrated bishops together some thirty-six years later. Bishop Abramowicz once said that "Mike had never met a Pole, and I had never met an Irishman. We were immediately attracted to each other."

Working in the cafeteria promised to be most enjoyable to Mike. His assignment was to serve soup from behind a long steam-table as the students walked by selecting their food. Mike considered this a great opportunity to become acquainted with everyone right from the start of the school year.

He was pleased to find that all of his professors were priests; and he immediately delved vigorously into his studies. Learning Latin especially fascinated him because it was the language of the Mass.

Having been a public school student, Mike had never had the privilege of being an altar boy. Now he obtained an instruction book and taught himself the Latin responses so that he could serve Mass. He volunteered as a Sunday acolyte at our parish church.

Very soon afterwards, and probably only because he was one of the smaller freshmen, Mike was asked to be a train-bearer for the Apostolic Delegate, Archbishop Amleto Cicognani, when the archbishop walked in procession into Holy Name Cathedral. Our family was elated by the honor of having our new server already on the altar at the cathedral with a visiting papal delegate.

By Christmas of Mike's first year in Quigley, our family funds were depleted. Dad had been unsuccessful in finding any kind of employment. Our landlord, Harry Dubnow, offered to trust us indefinitely when we could no longer pay rent.

It was then that the Ryans, who were still occupying the family home on Logan Boulevard, invited us to live with them. We accepted their kind invitation, and we moved in with Aunt Dais, Uncle Mage, and Uncle Bob.

Our uncles held political jobs which were not threatened by the national economic situation. Mage worked in City Hall and Bob was employed in the County Building.

They had always been very good to us children. Through the years they had provided us with the spending money which we happily disbursed for movies, candy, and street-car fare. It surely must have been a great sacrifice on their part to share their home with another family, as they were unaccustomed to the natural commotion of young people. As for us, during our stay with them we had our fill of the best of food; but we really felt the discomfort of losing the freedom of our own home.

Our aunt and uncles had a great respect for the priesthood, and they were proud of the fact that their nephew was a seminarian. Aunt Dais arranged a quiet place in the back of the house where Mike could study every evening undisturbed by the sound of the radio. Meanwhile, the rest of the family gathered around the console radio in the living room. "The Lone Ranger," Mollie Goldberg, and the quiz programs provided us with enjoyable entertainment.

We had been living with the Ryans for a year when Mollie Doyle, who was an old friend of the family, heard of our financial predicament and offered to open her vacant house on Francisco Avenue for us. She was unconcerned about rent money. Any small amount our parents could afford out of Dad's unemployment check from his union would be sufficient.

Mollie was a retired telephone operator. She was a little eccentric, but precious. Twenty years previously she had abandoned this home because her mother had been tragically burned to death in a fire that had swept through the basement. At the time of the fire, Dad had been at the firehouse, and, recognizing the address, had jumped on the engine and been the first to find Mrs. Doyle. He easily understood why Mollie never lived there again.

We happily accepted Mollie's offer and we soon moved to 2729 North Francisco Avenue, just a few blocks from the Ryans, and into St. Francis Xavier's parish again. Although the stone front of Mollie's house had held up very well with the years, the cracked plaster ceilings and the peeling painted walls within gave it a dilapidated appearance. Nevertheless, our new home looked very inviting. Spring was approaching, and the abundant tall trees which formed an arch along our residential street promised a lovely setting in the months to come.

Since leaving Barnes-Crosby, Dad had been working every part-time job he could find. He had been employed in some Public Works Administration projects while we were still living with the Ryans. The government had created the Public Works Administration, or PWA. This agency planned needed public works and made contracts with private companies. The cities and states joined to finance the projects that the agency approved. Dad was available to replace photoengravers who might be on sick leave;

but photoengraving was practically obsolete. Anne Flynn, who lived across the street from us, graciously received Dad's calls for work, because we had no telephone.

Mike was still working for his tuition at Quigley. By this time he had been promoted to cashier in the cafeteria. Many years later, one of his colleagues, Father Robert Burns, told us jokingly, "They had to promote Mike because the soup was selling for only a penny a bowl and Mike was losing money for the school by filling the bowls so full."

This would not have been too surprising because my brother dearly loved his classmates. I can remember seeing him wipe the tears from his eyes when he brought home the news that someone had left school, or was dismissed for being unable to keep up with the difficult studies.

It was in Mollie's house that Mike converted the closet in his bedroom into a chapel. The altar was more elaborate than the one he had made when he was a child. A vigil light glimmering against the statue of the Blessed Mother, and a red velvet-covered kneeler just fitting into the small room created a cozy place of retreat. Mike spent much time there in prayer.

By the end of the 1934 school year, we were very anxious to see the World's Fair, called A Century of Progress, which was being reopened on Chicago's lake front. We had seen only a small part of it the first year.

When he heard that there was to be a Children's Day at the fair, Mike volunteered to take all the children in our block, as we were already well acquainted with the neighbors. So when the day arrived, all the children gathered early in the morning with their bus fare, admission money, and lunches.

Apparently every child in Chicago had heard about the free rides and attractions being offered that day, because we waited in a seemingly endless line of people before we passed through the gates into the spacious fairgrounds. Entering from the north gate was Mike's plan, and we would see it all. He knew the names of the free attractions and found them all as we made our way through the crowds.

Eating lunch at large umbrella-covered tables was a real delight to our friends, and Mike counted heads every time we moved on again.

The Hall of States was probably the most enchanting place of all for us. None of us had had the opportunity to travel. Here we could see the forty-eight states represented in such a real setting that we could pretend we were traveling across the country as we selected a state and then leisurely walked through that state's exhibit. When we arrived at California and saw that the entrance was carved through the center of a giant redwood tree, we were sure that this would be the "greatest." The splashing waterfalls and the beautiful growing flowers charmed us; and the colorful lighted scenes on the walls depicting the places of interest in California were overwhelming in our estimation.

Evening came, and our group, still being counted by Mike, walked on, a little weary but not wanting to miss a bit of the "fantasy-land" kind of picture that the brilliantly-illuminated fair created against the darkening lake front.

Everyone had a magnificent time. Meanwhile, the radio news was reporting that there were numerous children lost and waiting at the fair gates. That was probably the reason that, when the bus stopped at Francisco Avenue late that warm night, there were many parents waiting, a little worried, but eager to hear the account of the day's happenings.

Mike's notable attraction to children was already obvious. As summer went on, he decided to do something constructive with the group of children who gathered on our front steps, so he wrote a play. It was entitled *Louisa Finds the Thief*. The characters were to acquire German accents. He created a part for everyone who wanted to be on stage. A box of antiquated clothes that Mollie's family had left behind made beautiful costumes. Preparing and producing this play in our basement, as well as selling two-cent admission tickets, kept many children, including the Dempseys, happy for weeks.

Then summer ended, Mike's seventeenth birthday came, and we were back in school again. But winter was on the way, and we had not anticipated its added hardships for the people who were poor.

The winter of 1934-35 was a cold one, and our heating was not adequate. Even with coal burning in the furnace, the house could never be sufficiently warm. There were times when our supply of coal would be exhausted and Dad had to chop up old unused doors that he found in the basement, and burn them in order to produce some amount of heat. Often the house was so cold that Mike would study sitting in bed with his blankets around him and with heavy gloves on his hands.

Mother and Mike were both getting asthma attacks more frequently. Because of his illness Mike would sometimes miss several
days of school, but he never let this discourage him in any way.

It had been necessary for us to apply for public aid — then
called Relief. When the Relief truck stopped in front of our house,
it brought with it a real blow to our parents' pride. Probably it was
even harder for Mom to accept because she had grown up in the
days when the Ryans were well up the ladder of affluence. We
surely needed and used the canned food that was delivered to us,
but it was not usually the kind of food we would have selected.
The clothing was drab, and the size was the only thing left to our
choosing. However, Dad always promised us that our living conditions would improve, and we believed him. Dad's optimism was a
great asset.

Eventually spring came and summer followed; and, when we
warmed up, the whole world looked brighter. The fragrance of the
lilacs in our back yard and the sounds of summer coming through
our open windows were a delight to all. Our front stairway was
crowded with neighborhood children who came to call for Agnes
and Kathryn, and to play games of guessing movie stars' names.
Everyone was in good spirits.

Our parents' spirits were enhanced by a little light in view at
the long end of the tunnel of Depression. A new newspaper was in
the process of development. This alone gave evidence of an im-
proving economy. It was to be the first tabloid in the Chicago area
and was described as the small newspaper that would be easy to
read on a street car. Dad knew many people in the newspaper
business who would be glad to give him a recommendation
because he was a skilled photoengraver. He was counting on this.
He was interviewed at the *Daily Times*, and offered a two-day
week initially, with the promise of a full week as soon as the new
tabloid would "catch on" with the public. He also got an assurance that he would grow rapidly with it.

Then the telegram came, calling Dad back to work at his own
trade. Though Mike was young, he knew the meaning of a good
job; and recognizing the telegram as our ticket to a better life, he
tacked it up on our living room wall.

The newspaper met with success. Eventually Dad became
foreman of the engraving department, and he remained with the
Daily Times the rest of his life. In future years, a huge new plant
was built on the Chicago River opposite the original site. The

newspaper is presently known as the *Sun Times.*

By the end of that summer, Mother was expressing her concern about Michael's passing the strict physical examination which
was required for entrance into the major seminary. Although this
physical wouldn't be given immediately, she already had some
qualms about the possibility that a doctor could find Michael
suffering from asthma, and thereby deem it necessary to disqualify
him.

When Mom was very young and really incapacitated because
of asthma, her brother John had taken her to Denver with the expectation that the change in climate might give her some relief.
Upon stepping off the train in the high altitude of the beautiful
mountainland, she could breathe again, and was free of asthma for
the next eleven years. Any time Mother would mention this, she
would add, "Always say a little prayer for John. He was so good
to me." Now she was longing for Michael to experience a similar
remission; and Dad developed an idea.

There was only one way to raise money for sending Mike on
a trip to the West. Dad could borrow on his own life insurance. He
had always kept his insurance a priority, and was in good standing
for a loan. Afer this was arranged, it took some convincing, but
Mike agreed to go. Soon he was on a train headed for Colorado.

Mike took with him a letter of introduction written by a
family friend, Father Martin, to a priest in Denver, who, Father
Martin said, would be glad to find a place for Mike to live for two
weeks.

It took the Denver priest only a half-hour's time, and he was
back to the rectory where Michael was waiting. His parishioners,
the Kienerrys, would be very pleased to have a seminarian for
their guest. This was the beginning of Mike's long-time friendship
with the Kienerrys. They treated him royally. Their relatives took
turns "borrowing" him for a day and showing him all the places
of interest in the city. Since Mike had never been away from the
lowlands of Illinois, viewing the gorgeous mountain scenery was
truly a delight.

At night the family dog would find his way into Mike's
room, and every morning Mike would awaken with the dog sleep-
ing next to him.

This vacation was a wonderful experience for my brother,
and he enjoyed every minute of it. Although it was not a cure for
his asthma, he had no symptoms when the day came for the

physical examination before graduation from Quigley, and he passed with flying colors.

We remained in Mollie's house for a year and a half; and after we left, she was never without tenants. Mollie always said that Michael Dempsey's chapel brought blessings to her house.

All the family truly appreciated the better life which Dad's job provided. We girls went on to The Immaculate High School, operated by the Sisters of Charity of the Blessed Virgin Mary. We had the opportunity for some time in college if we wished to continue in school. Agnes attended Wright College, and I attended Mundelein. Kay found her summer job in a bank so interesting that she decided to stay on there, instead of entering college.

"Growing up Irish" in Chicago meant that we had developed a pride in the land of our ancestry. Mother often said that Ireland was the home of poets and saints. We were familiar with all the Irish songs because our Sunday evening radio schedule always included "The Irish Hour," hosted by Maurice Lynch. But, I think that other than the fact that we ate potatoes with every dinner, that was the extent of the Irish influence on Mike.

Michael Dempsey at nineteen was a very happy young man who knew exactly what he wanted to do with his life. His transition from Quigley to St. Mary of the Lake would mean the end of his daily association with the family. We anticipated the loneliness; but we shared his dream of the priesthood. When Mike left home, we all went with him in spirit.

CHAPTER FOUR

TOWARD THE PRIESTHOOD

FOR YEARS MICHAEL had longed for the day when he would enter St. Mary of the Lake, the major seminary for the archdiocese. But parting was a heartache for him and for us. Dad, Mother, and the three of us girls went with him to the Belmont station of the North Shore Electric Line, where he and other seminarians boarded a special train for the journey to Mundelein.

We were unaware of the fact that Grandfather Dempsey had also boarded the train, but at another station. Since our grandfather was quite striking in appearance, he could hardly ride unnoticed. Though he was in his eighties, he still stood tall, and his beautiful white wavy hair added to his dignity. As he walked through the cars looking for his grandson, everyone warmly welcomed him; and the "stowaway" became the honored guest of the seminarians as the North Shore express rolled swiftly out of the city and through the open countryside.

The electric line did not customarily stop at the seminary entrance, except when the whole student body was returning to school. The sadness of leaving home quickly faded away as the classmates were reunited; and it was a happy and excited crowd of young men who stepped off the train. A truck was waiting to carry their suitcases and trunks. Grandfather walked across the road and to the entrance of the seminary grounds with Mike. After shaking many, many hands and wishing everyone success, he turned to his beloved grandson and said, "Mike, I came just to see you through the gates."

It was a long and winding road beyond the gates, and Grandfather stood silently watching until the last of the boys had disappeared from his view. Then he turned about, walked to the town of Libertyville, and waited for a train to Chicago.

As many occasions in our lives have a parallel, so this one did. Eight years later, on New Year's Eve, as our grandfather was dying, he anxiously waited for his own Father Mike to come to administer the sacraments to him, and "see him through the gates."

St. Mary of the Lake Seminary had been built by George Cardinal Mundelein in the early 1920s. Located forty miles northwest of Chicago, near the small town of Area, the seminary was the cardinal's great achievement. His seminarians were his prize possessions, and he wanted the best for them.

The stately-pillared chapel was centered by a pattern of matching buildings. The grounds were spacious, and the landscaping was elegant. A clear blue lake, beneath a turning staircase where remote sidewalks followed the Stations of the Cross, created an atmosphere of tranquility. Soon the town changed its name to Mundelein to honor the cardinal.

Cardinal Mundelein died in the fall of 1939. He was buried near the main altar of the seminary chapel where he had ordained his beloved priests.

In the major seminary every student wore a cassock and biretta. The students looked both professional and angelic in their clerical attire. Much was required of them. The studies were difficult, the discipline rigid.

My brother entered with a lively interest in practically everything the seminary had to offer. He never had been an athlete, but now he played baseball and loved it. Golf and tennis were among the other enjoyments the seminary grounds offered.

In the classroom Mike was greatly respected as a "real brain" who never wanted anyone to notice his brilliance. When no one else in the class knew the answer to a particular question, the professor would just turn to Mike Dempsey from whom he would be very sure of receiving a clear and correct answer. But Mike would not have raised his hand to offer a response.

As the years went by, the pursuit of knowledge was an increasing joy to Mike. He was ever generous in sharing his learning. Anyone who wanted to walk around the lake with him to get some difficult point in philosophy or theology clarified would be welcome to any amount of his time just for the asking.

One of Mike's classmates told me that he didn't think Mike ever broke a rule. He added, "Mike didn't do this out of any particular desire to impress anyone. It was just that he knew it was the thing to do and he did it."

During these years we observed that Mike's asthma was something that he accepted willingly; but he preferred that no one would notice or mention his discomfort. Thereafter, we respected his wishes.

In his days as a seminarian and throughout his lifetime, there was a significant sameness in his personality. He would always be the most quiet one in a group. Mike would sit, smiling pleasantly, and obviously enjoying every bit of the conversation, but his voice

was never heard above the crowd. I don't ever remember his utter-
ing a loud word. Nevertheless, people were drawn to him. His
gentle friendliness and his genuine interest in what others had to
say made people want to claim him as a friend. He never passed a
person on the street without some kind of recognition — a smile
or a "Hi."

During his summers at Mundelein, Mike worked in the library
on the campus. Since the library was one of his favorite places, his
work was a pleasure. Included in his duties was escorting visitors
on tours of the buildings. One building that was particularly interesting was the museum. It housed a collection of ecclesiastical
souvenirs from all of our Chicago cardinals and bishops.

Michael wrote home frequently from school and he related
all the interesting happenings. On one occasion when there was a
big football game and the teams played pranks on one another, he
had an amusing story to share with us — about cassocks attached
to window sills and blowing in the wind like black flags. Sometimes his letters were very funny; for instance, the time that he
accidentally bumped into a bees' nest and had to run with swarms
of bees buzzing after him.

It was a long road to the priesthood and much sacrifice was
required of the seminarians. Visiting was restricted to one Sunday
afternoon each month. Our friend, John Mancuso, always drove us
to Mundelein on that day. Each student was allowed only three
visitors, and they sat in little clusters in the classrooms. The
remaining family members who came would enjoy walking along
the lake shore until the three o'clock chimes signaled the end of
the visiting time. Then they would wait for a brief greeting with
their own seminarian and the other students. Through the years
the families became friends as they shared the happiness of re-
union, the sadness of separation, and the vision of a great ordination day.

The seminarians remained in school during the holidays. The
loneliness of being away from their families at Christmas was
tempered by the expectation of two weeks at home in January.
Many parents, including our own, looked forward to this time
when they would invite a houseful of their son's classmates to
dinner. It was always a merry group and they delighted in being
together. The mainstream of conversation centered about
seminary life; but then the boys would get Dad to talk about the
newspaper business. Mother could be sure that her homemade pies

were appreciated by them all.

Of course, relatives and friends who took much pride in their seminarian expected to see him during this vacation; so it was a constant whirl of visiting. Then the boys were back to the routine of hard study until June.

In their later years in the seminary, Mike and his classmates, Jack Egan and Jerry Weber, regularly spent an hour every Thursday morning in the basement of the chapel, where they practiced what they called "homiletics." They prepared speeches or sermons and then criticized one another as they tried to improve their voices, their delivery, and their gestures. This was a valuable training experience for all of them. Mike was ever faithful to this appointment and he was always very kind in making any criticism.

Michael was home on vacation in August of 1940 when our family moved into a large second-floor apartment at 2857 Logan Boulevard. It was there that our mother and father lived the rest of their lives. Now we were back in St. Sylvester's where our parents had been married and where we had been baptized. Our parents felt that their roots were in St. Sylvester's and they wanted their son to celebrate his first Mass in that church.

Mike went to the rectory to register the family and to introduce himself as a seminarian. There he met Father Philip Cahill, who had been assigned to the parish since his ordination a few years before.

Father Cahill graciously welcomed Michael; and he arranged to meet all of us very soon afterwards. This was the beginning of our long-time association with Father Cahill, whom we quickly claimed as an additional member of our family.

Some months before ordination, there was a wonderful surprise in store for my brother. Thomas O'Brien, the president of the Peoples' Gas Company union, intended to donate a chalice, in memory of his deceased mother, to some young man who would be ordained the following May. Our cousin, Laura Burns, happened to know of this, and without informing us, she interceded in Mike's behalf. When a chauffeur delivered the beautiful chalice to our door, Dad, a little tearful, accepted it as a gift dropped out of the skies. (After Mother's death in 1951, the diamond from her engagement ring was implanted in the center of the Gaelic cross which adorned the chalice. This had been her request.)

It was 1943; the country was at war. Although no one from our immediate household was in service, practically all the young men we knew were away. But the Dempsey family was looking forward to May 1, when Mike would be ordained by Samuel Cardinal Stritch, who had succeeded Cardinal Mundelein in 1939.

Then the long-awaited day for ordination came. It was as joyous a day as we had anticipated. By six-thirty in the morning our relatives and friends were gathering at our door. Springtime and sunshine and our elated spirits combined to enhance the beauty of the country scene, as we traveled the familiar roads to Mundelein.

Witnessing the Church's solemn traditional ceremonies of ordination, as Cardinal Stritch conferred the sacrament of holy orders on the young men whom we knew so well, was indeed a memorable experience for each of us; and our own Mike was a priest forever.

Then, as the clear loud tones of the chimes ringing from high above the chapel resounded throughout the seminary grounds, all those present walked about in the fragrant green grass and knelt at the feet of each newly-ordained priest to receive his first blessing.

On the following day, Sunday, Michael celebrated his First Mass at our parish church. A mood of exultation permeated St. Sylvester's that morning. It seemed to have continued from the preceding Sunday's Easter ceremonies. The elegance of the altar and the sparkling gold vestments was enhanced by the excellence of the choir. For our family and the many relatives and friends who had waited through the years to participate in Michael's First Mass, it was a dream fulfilled. We saw our own joy reflected in the faces of those who greeted us throughout this day of celebration.

One humorous touch was added to our memories of the occasion. After all the guests had gathered at Logan Square's Terminal Restaurant for the banquet, we realized that Father Michael was not present. Father Cahill, who was to be the master of ceremonies, drove back to St. Sylvester's and found Mike standing in front of the rectory. Mike laughed as he explained that while he had gone back for his vestment bag, the last cars had driven away.

CHAPTER FIVE

THE TRAINING GROUND

AFTER ORDINATION, ALL of the new priests had a short vacation at home while they awaited the official announcement of their appointments. Michael offered Mass at St. Sylvester's early each morning. On one of these spring mornings, as he walked to church, he was taken by surprise when a man came running out from his house saying, "Father, my mother is dying. Will you come in to her?"

Mike immediately administered the sacrament of the dying to the elderly lady. Only three days after ordination he had been called upon to extend his priestly services.

During their vacation the classmates spent much time together, golfing and playing tennis. Michael would usually be back home long before dinner. When Kay returned from school, and when Agnes and I came in from work late in the afternoon, our first words would be, "Where's Mike?"

Invariably Mom answered, "He's been out on the front porch for over an hour with his pen and paper. Just let him be alone." We knew that, in his youthful fervor, he was praying and planning and jotting down ideas in his eagerness to begin the Lord's work.

It was an exciting day when the mailman rang our bell to personally deliver Cardinal Stritch's letter. The forty new priests must have been at their phones all day long, as they happily compared notes on their assignments. Father John O'Connell and Father Mike Dempsey were the only ones assigned to special duty. They were to return to the seminary for post-graduate work leading to a doctorate in theology. Mike had not expected this kind of assignment, but he was immediately willing and enthused about it.

The other classmates joked about the "long and the short of it" when referring to the contrast in appearance of the two. John was light-haired and tall, while Mike was dark-haired and short. However, they were a fine pair and thoroughly enjoyed being together. It was a year of hard work for them. The research was endless, and the composing and rewriting required their utmost efforts.

As seminarians, they had been exempt from military service. Now, after ordination, the young priests were free to volunteer their time for chaplain duty. Father John and Father Mike were near enough to Great Lakes Naval Base in Waukegan to spend weekends with the servicemen. This opportunity to become acquainted with men from every part of the country was a most enjoyable experience for them. They offered Mass in the Navy chapel and were available for long hours in the confessional.

When spring came, their post-graduate work was completed, and the two classmates awaited the results. Father John received his STD; Father Mike did not. The professor who judged Mike's thesis said that there was something, which he couldn't put into words, that was missing from Mike's dissertation. Mike was crushed. He sincerely felt that he had been treated unjustly. He thought that he should have been informed of any inadequacies along the way, instead of receiving a last-minute rejection.

He made a special trip home to talk to Mother. They sat at the kitchen table, broken-hearted, but resigned. Then Mike took the train back to the seminary where he visited with Father Motherway, a Jesuit professor. The priest was very sympathetic, but he assured Mike that there was only one way to interpret this terrible disappointment.

"Mike," he said, "if you had a doctorate in theology you might not be doing parish work. There is something that God has for you to do that you wouldn't be able to do in a classroom." That was all Mike needed. He returned home joyfully to await his assignment to a parish; and he never again mentioned this disappointment.

When the cardinal's letter came, assigning him to St. Mary of the Lake Church on Sheridan Road, Mike couldn't have been happier. We were familiar with the church. Although it had the same name as the seminary, the two were not connected. The church was impressively large, ornate, and beautiful in appearance. Since this parish was less than five miles from home, Mike could just "hop" a bus on his day off, and hopefully we would see him often.

He would indeed be riding the buses for a long time, since a priest was not allowed to own a car until five years after ordination; and we had no family car. Each priest was expected to pay a debt to the seminary before taking on the expense which owning a car would entail. The archdiocese, with the help of some generous people supported the seminary at Mundelein, and students did not pay tuition. After ordination the young priests sent one hundred dollars annually for five years to the cardinal, to repay, in token at least, the cost of their education.

So it was in early June that young Father Dempsey walked into his new home to meet his pastor, the elderly Monsignor John Dennison, and the other associate priests. Father Edward Cardinal was one of the priests he met. Father Cardinal recalls, "It was my good fortune to have been in residence at St. Mary of the Lake Rectory when the pastor introduced to us his newly-ordained assistant. It was a most pleasant and memorable presentation. Why? He had such a smile — a smile that reflected a magnetic and charming personality. It was not a manufactured smile but one that reflected a quiet and peaceful interior. It was such a precious asset that it would win for him countless souls for Christ."

Father Dempsey was the essence of vitality when he assumed his many duties as the youngest priest at St. Mary's. His rooms were on the third floor of the old but elegant rectory. This would be his home for eighteen years. Here he had a spacious setting for his collection of books. Books were very important to him, and he was constantly learning. Included in his library was a book which he had recently purchased. He was very happy to have come upon it in a bookstore. I don't recall the title, but it was the biography of Father Tim Dempsey, a parish priest in St. Louis, who had done much social work in the community in which he lived. It is very likely that Father Tim's life made a deep impression on Mike.

Within the parish boundaries lived people of various social and economic classes. The rich lived to the east of the church in high-rise apartments overlooking the lake or in spacious homes. In sharp contrast, west of the church the poorer people lived in deteriorating apartment houses. The neighborhood north of St. Mary's was gradually changing to be a community inhabited by American Indians and whites from Appalachia.

Intermingled were Spanish-speaking people whose presence immediately motivated Mike to study the language so that he could fulfill the need for a Spanish-speaking confessor. This interest eventually led him to the Cardinal's Committee for Spanish-Speaking People.

As Father Cardinal said, "The face of the city was changing, and the neighborhood changed with it. Father Dempsey was young enough to envisage the problems and to become a part of them. Because of his personality he was able to retain the confidence of the old and to win the esteem and affection of the new."

Michael was very anxious to meet his flock. Each Sunday morning as the chimes from St. Mary's announced the beginning of another Mass, he would stand in front of the church and greet the people.

It didn't take long for the children to find him. His friendly manner acted as a magnet. When school opened in September he began teaching them religion. Occasionally, as a reward for having learned their catechism well, he gave the children nickels and dimes; for some of the youngsters this was a real incentive.

They followed him everywhere; and he gave his time generously to them. He still enjoyed the boyish pleasure of a baseball workout in the park at Montrose Beach, and the children began calling the hill in the park "Father Dempsey's Hill."

As time went on, it wasn't difficult for my brother to decide which boys he should invite along on his summer vacation. He easily found a few who would not be having the advantage of a family vacation. The chance to give these youngsters a great time was Father Dempsey's idea of a two-week holiday.

The young priest had a diversity of interests in his parish. He considered the instruction of prospective converts a very basic duty, and he was available at any hour for those who asked for instructions. His converts were many, and often they became his close friends. Long after his death some of these friends still brought flowers to his grave.

Mike was greatly devoted to the sick and the dying, and he always found time to visit with our family's sick relatives and friends. He brought the sacraments and kindness and sympathy to the St. Mary's people, whether they were in American Hospital, which the parish priests serviced, or confined at home. Mom was very proud to wear the beautiful aprons which his elderly ladies made for her.

On one occasion, our friend, Virginia Mersch, called to tell us that her father had been killed when he jumped from his burning third-floor apartment near St. Mary's Church. Virginia was anxious to know if her father had had the happiness of receiving the sacrament of the dying. We reached Michael on the phone, and he assured us that he had been on the scene at three o'clock in the morning and had annointed Virginia's father on the sidewalk before he died. (Mike was always tuned in to the sound of fire alarms in the night – an awareness fostered by our Grandfather Dempsey and our father, who sometimes awakened us children in the middle of the night to go with him to a fire.)

Mundelein College for Women was located on Sheridan Road

just a few miles north of St. Mary of the Lake Church. A unique
"skyscraper college" for women, its campus overlooked the shores
of Lake Michigan. Sister Ann Ida, the college president, asked
Father Dempsey to teach a Bible course to seniors. This subject
was dear to him. Since he viewed her request as an added opportunity for priestly work, and the short teaching hours would not
interfere with his parish duties, he readily accepted with his
pastor's permission. Teaching was a joy. He commented that there
was no effort in maintaining attention in college. Everyone was
there because she wanted to be.

"He always came through as a scholar," Sister Catherine remembers. "What I admired most about him was that he was
always himself, a very gentle man." She added that no student
went to Father Dempsey's class to be entertained. Scripture was a
very serious subject.

Mike had such a great esteem for the Bible and he knew it so
completely that he was an inspiration to his students. His future
ministry would provide a literal example of the life Christ taught
in the New Testament: the Lord did not remain in the temple;
rather, He went out among the people. Years later, one of his
former students said, "Now I understand why Father Dempsey
would ask his classes to calculate the distance the Lord walked
on each occasion."

Another student recalled the deep understanding my brother
had of the apostles. "St. Paul was Father Dempsey's favorite," she
said. "Father Dempsey felt sorry for Paul because the other
apostles didn't completely trust him, since he had persecuted the
Christians before his conversion. For this reason Paul often
traveled alone to preach."

Probably no one in Mundelein College would have predicted
that the professor who taught the Bible would eventually become
a bishop, because Mike Dempsey was an unusually quiet man.
Surely it was the gentleness and approachability which characterized him in the classroom that won him the confidence and love of
his students. He was equally approachable by persons of any age.
Everyone could feel comfortable with him. He appeared to con-
verse with the most educated person in the same tone in which he
spoke to a small child.

Aside from the spiritual aspect of teaching the Bible, this
teaching position provided him with a regular salary which he in
turn applied to the payment of Catholic high school tuition for

some of his young parishioners whose parents could not afford this expense. This was something Mike never mentioned at home; but, through the years, people told us stories about his special concern for the education of their youngsters.

His concern for the young brought him many added responsibilities. Often neighborhood boys who were considered juvenile delinquents were paroled to him and were required to report to him weekly at the rectory. Many times Mike would spend hours waiting in Children's Memorial Hospital with some parents whose child was seriously ill. He could always spare the time if someone needed his support.

Father Tom Purtell recalls an incident some years later, when he and Mike were both stationed at Our Lady of Lourdes on the Westside. Father Purtell was upstairs in his room about nine o'clock one evening when he heard Michael coming into the rectory. Mike, apparently fatigued, ascended the stairway very slowly. He greeted Father Tom and then said, "I'm going to read a little bit and then go to bed." And he closed his door.

At eleven-thirty, the phone rang and Father Purtell answered. It was Father Ed Conway, of St. Mary of the Lake, calling from American Hospital to say that a neighborhood boy had been stabbed during a fight. "They're operating on him now. I annointed him and he's all set. But he wanted to see Father Dempsey," the priest said.

This was one of the boys about whom Mike used to say, "I bounced him on my knee."

Father Purtell said, "He's dead to the world now, Ed."

Father Conway answered, "Well, just let him know. I promised the kid I'd inform Father Dempsey that he's all set — had the sacraments."

Father Purtell assured him that he would, and then he buzzed Michael's room. Mike picked up the phone.

"Mike," Father Tom said, "Eddie Conway called about this guy," and he mentioned his name. "He was in a knife fight. But he's gonna make it. He's been annointed and he's in the operating room now; but the kid just wanted to make sure that you knew about it."

"Okay, thanks," Mike answered.

Five minutes later, the door opened, and Mike was down the stairs and out to his car. It was three hours later when he returned, and again he climbed the stairs one at a time.

"That was typical of Mike," Father Purtell added. "He probably knew the boy's mother would be there waiting."

On another occasion, a woman who was in an unhappy marriage went to St. Mary's rectory to ask Father Dempsey's counsel. Not only was the young priest very concerned, but on the following day he appeared at her door asking to speak to her husband. "My husband treated him ruthlessly," she said. "But the fact that Father Dempsey came out to approach him was very important to me."

Mike's first four years at St. Mary's had been happy for him; he was doing the work he loved. We were very proud of him and considered ourselves fortunate to have him close to home. He could continue to take part in momentous family events, both happy and sad.

The year 1948 was an eventful one for our family. On January 17, Dad died at the age of fifty-eight. He had been on sick leave from the newspaper for two months because of a heart condition. Mike offered the funeral Mass, but he told me afterwards that he shouldn't have attempted reading the prayers at the graveside because it was so hard to do.

During Dad's illness Michael had permission to say Mass twice in our home. Dad shed tears of joy when he had the privilege of serving his son's Mass. No doubt it brought back memories of his little boy "playing" Mass.

Dad's death was especially difficult, because the first wedding in the family was to take place on the following Saturday. Agnes was marrying Charles Brown. Of course Mike was officiating, as he would be at all the family weddings in the future. Dad had urged them to proceed with their plans and to have a wonderful day. The dinner at the restaurant was cancelled; but Aunt Dais served us a fine meal. Mother really depended on Michael for support that day, and he was a great comfort to her.

Then, there was another wedding scheduled for the 26th of June. My dear husband, Jack Burke, and I were married on that day. Since this was some months after Dad's death, it was a much happier occasion than Agnes' and Charlie's wedding had been.

Mike was most pleased to welcome his two brothers-in-law into the family. He accompanied the four of us on many outings that summer.

By the time that Kay married in September of 1950, the Browns had two babies, and we had one. Kay married Bill Hastings, the brother of our friends, Marge and Eileen Hastings; and this marriage united not only the young couple, but the two families.

Marge had married Edward Kane, and Eileen was to marry Clarence Jacobs. They, and the Hastings brothers, James and Pat, their wives, June and Myra, and all the children who followed were fondly called our "cousins' cousins," and our clan grew rapidly.

Meanwhile, at St. Mary's, Mike was becoming more and more involved in community affairs. In many respects Uptown proved to be the training ground where he prepared for his great commitment to the poor. The Uptown neighborhood, extending along Broadway Avenue, was becoming a community filled with recently-migrated people who needed help in becoming urbanized. Housing costs frequently forced two or three families to share one apartment. Job skills were an urgent need. The non-profit day-labor concept had been discussed for several years by residents and community workers who believed that Uptown's flourishing day-labor industry created a "slave-labor" situation.

Firms maintained agreements with job suppliers not to hire day-laborers on a permanent basis within ninety days after they were sent out on a job. By moving the laborers from company to company each day, the day-labor offices could effectively shut unskilled workers out of permanent employment.

Despite the known constraints of the day-labor system, many people, especially recent migrants to the city, had to become involved in it simply because they couldn't wait a week or two for the first paycheck on a permanent job.

The employment situation was then, and continued to be in future years, one of Father Dempsey's prime involvements. Remembering our own father's lack of work in the Depression days of the 1930s, Mike never forgot the flavor of poverty.

Hull House was considering opening a new outpost in the area, and the director of Hull House invited representatives of the various ethnic groups, social agencies, and parishes in Uptown to attend a meeting, the purpose of which was to determine the extent of the need for such an outpost in that particular community.

Father Peter Powell, the resident clergyman of St. Augustine's Indian Center, in Uptown, sat and listened as young Father Dempsey rose to speak. "He mentioned St. Mary's parish itself only briefly," Father Powell recalls. "Instead, he spoke of the differing needs of the many people living in the community: Appalachian whites, Spanish-speaking people, native Americans, Blacks, run-of-the-mill Anglo-Saxons, old residents, and new-comers. Clearly his concern was for all of them, and he spoke quietly but movingly of their need to keep their own identities while finding lives of dignity and satisfaction right there in Up-town. He spoke of the role Hull House should play in such a com-munity; and especially of how the Hull House professional staff must be willing to listen to the people and heed them, serving those needs the people themselves saw as being important, rather than imposing professional programs by professional outsiders upon Uptown's citizens. 'If Hull House could operate with this type of sensitivity, then the new outpost could be of real value to the community,' Father Dempsey declared.

"Hull House came, and during Father Dempsey's years at St. Mary of the Lake, continued to demonstrate the sensitivity he de-scribed that day," Father Powell continued. "I am convinced that Father Dempsey's speech, coupled with his obviously intimate knowledge of the needs of the many races who formed Uptown, were key factors in Hull House's decision to build a permanent neighborhood center there."

In many ways my brother's influence was felt in Uptown long after he left the community.

The 1950s were a decade of growth for the Church in the Archdiocese of Chicago. The Second World War had ended and the boys were back to begin new lives. They were finding jobs, marrying, beginning their families; and they were anxious to invest in homes of their own. Suburban communities developed rapidly. Cardinal Stritch assigned many priests to the task of establishing new suburban parishes. This included the building of parish schools. I remember Mike's commenting that it was much too hard a job for one man — to go out and build a parish.

An increased enrollment in Catholic high schools resulted in the erecting of many beautiful schools in the Chicago area, as well as the enlarging of many of the older high school buildings, includ-ing our Immaculata. (A decade later, the Church couldn't keep pace with the move to the suburbs. Parishes were established with-out parochial schools.)

The Church was concentrating on family life. Pre-Cana con-ferences (counseling prior to marriage) were conducted for en-gaged couples; Cana conferences (counseling after marriage) followed; and the Christian Family Movement was flourishing.

Cardinal Stritch died in May of 1958. He was succeeded by Archbishop Albert Meyer. The following year the archbishop was made a cardinal.

During all this time Mike remained at St. Mary's, although it was customary for the cardinal to transfer his priests every few years. I have no idea why Michael was assigned to one parish for so long. After the first few years Mother used to say, "I think Monsignor Dennison has asked to keep him. The monsignor always says, 'He's the sunshine of our house.'" But the monsignor was long gone, and Mike stayed on.

Occasionally someone would remark, "Mike, the cardinal forgot where you are. You'll stay there forever." Mike would smile as though nothing would please him more.

In June of 1962, Michael received a letter from Cardinal Meyer — it was a notice of transfer from St. Mary of the Lake to St. Francis De Paula on the Southside. Everyone was taken by surprise. For Michael, leaving his parish would be another experience in leaving home.

The parishioners wanted to give him a loving and memorable "send-off," and they accomplished this to the utmost. Ruth and John Cleaveland planned the reception. The Cleavelands and their crew created a "This Is Your Life, Father Dempsey" (patterned after the popular television show of that time), to be enacted in the St. Mary's auditorium.

Father Michael sat in a large chair on the stage and watched as a succession of old and not-so-old friends and relatives came forward to recount their memories of him. Uncle Bob Ryan was the oldest friend of the guest of honor. When Jack and I with our seven small children, Agnes and Charlie with their seven, and Kay and Bill and their five little ones, were called upon, we filled most of the stage.

Then some of Mike's early life was recalled, including the story about the time our neighbor, Mrs. Eisenschimel, rushed to our kitchen door carrying our baby sister who had fallen down the back stairway. Little Kathryn had become so frightened that she held her breath and was turning blue. "Mike, throw some water in her face," our neighbor shouted. Mike obediently dashed to the sink, filled a glass with water, and in his excitement, threw the water smack into Mrs. Eisenschimel's face. After the laughter subsided, and the redness in Mike's face as well, he quickly recognized with a smile the voices of classmates, who told humorous anecdotes from behind stage.

Several young people wanted to tell their friend, Father Dempsey, that he had greatly influenced their lives. Kathy Mancuso, whose father had taken us to the seminary on visiting Sundays for many years, appeared because she was the first person Father Dempsey had baptized. Now she was asking him to officiate at her wedding.

Firemen who had been on many fire scenes with him were there.

Captain Fahey of the local Town Hall District, as well as other police officers with whom Mike had worked on juvenile problems, or who had repeatedly met him at American Hospital with accident victims, had interesting remembrances to relate.

The captain presented Father Dempsey with a pair of gold cuff-links which bore the emblem of the Chicago Police Department. (These cuff-links were much later presented to Officer Edward Kane when he married our daughter, Maureen.)

The entertainment committee had even delved into the parish statistics, so that they could inform Father Dempsey that he had baptized seventeen hundred and sixty-one people and had married six hundred and four couples.

Finally everyone had appeared on stage. Michael, seeming to be at a loss for words, beamed with happiness; for this was truly a tribute of love.

CHAPTER SIX

AN UNCLE CALLED FATHER D

AT THE TIME that Charlie Brown came into the family, he began calling our brother "Father D." Charlie was such a pleasant fellow that probably any name he could have chosen for his brother-in-law would have sounded as well; but somehow, the name "Father D" caught on with all of us very quickly. From then on, every one of us affectionately called Michael by that name; and our children knew him by no other.

The baptisms of our babies were always happy occasions. Father D saw his own christening dress used many, many times, as his nieces and nephews each had a turn to wear it on the day he baptized them. Dear Aunt Dais was eighty years old, and the dress was paper-thin, when she again whitened it, and sewed on new bows and ribbons for the last child in the second generation who wore it. As each little one grew old enough to become aware of the people around him, he recognized Father D as someone "special" and someone who loved him very much.

Holidays brought the whole Dempsey clan, including many in-laws, together for a big dinner party. Thanksgiving Day was the day we Burkes traditionally hosted the celebration.

In one of the earlier years, Father D arrived on Thanksgiving with a new movie camera and took pictures of the babies. This was the beginning of a hobby at which he became very proficient. In the succeeding years he made a collection of movies that were precious, and sometimes hilarious; and the value of these family scenes ever increased. No one enjoyed these movies any more than Father D himself.

He was definitely the unifying force in our family. All of our activities were scheduled according to his availability, not because he would expect any special consideration, but because his being present made everyone happier. No doubt it was his simple holiness that attracted us. He had an ability to make each of us feel important and successful, whether it was a small child learning to walk, or a parent whose family was growing in wisdom and grace.

Father D ever retained his youthful enthusiasm for picnics, and a family picnic for him was his special day with the children. It was always a memorable one. He would bring a box filled with small prizes; and he would delight in conducting the races. Our "cousins' cousins," the Jacobs, the Kanes, and other Hastings families would be with us, making our group very large.

After the games, he would let the little children bury him in the sand on the beach. Then they would pull him to the water and dunk him.

Rather than taking part in the exciting baseball game, he would prefer to be far out on the lake in a small boat with a few of the youngsters blissfully rowing him. At the end of the day he would relax in a lounge chair. The children would be on his lap, on the arms of his chair, and at his feet.

Though parish duties kept Father D constantly busy, he was ever aware of and concerned about any family problems that would arise. When I was expecting our daughter, Eileen, I happened to have a difficult pregnancy which necessitated my remaining in bed for some weeks. One afternoon, my brother stopped in unexpectedly for a brief visit and blessed me with his relics. Immediately after he left, our first-grader, Tom, returned from school. I told Tom that he had just missed seeing his uncle, and that I had been blessed with three relics.

Tom said, "Oh, I know that."

Then I asked him if he had seen Father D's car from the school window.

"No," Tom replied, "but at lunchtime I went into church and asked God to bless you and the baby; so He sent Father D with the blessing."

I remember how happy Father D was when we moved into our two-flat building on Addison Street with Jack's family, his mother and uncle, and his brother Dick. Michael came immediately to bless every room upstairs and downstairs.

Eventually the Browns and the Hastings left Chicago. Charlie and Agnes and their family moved into a newly-built home in Schaumburg. Bill and Kay and their five children moved fifty miles out of Chicago, to Ingleside, near Fox Lake. Their home was situated in a beautiful rural setting, one block uphill from a chain of lakes. Father D shared in their happiness, and he appreciated any hours he could spend with them, away from the excitement of the big city.

CHAPTER SEVEN

INTO THE BLACK COMMUNITY

SOON AFTER MICHAEL received his transfer from St. Mary of the Lake, he was moving into the rectory at 78th and Dobson Streets. He was to be an assistant to Father McHugo, the pastor of St. Francis De Paula Church.

This appointment brought Mike into an established and quite affluent neighborhood in the Avalon area. The proximity of the Chatham Station of the Illinois Central Railroad made it attractive to people who commuted to jobs downtown. However, its beautiful and expensive apartment buildings attracted adult residents, so that children comprised only about one-tenth of the population.

Consequently, St. Francis' School had a relatively small enrollment. At the time Michael arrived there, Father Frank Phelan, the pastor of St. Thaddeus (at 95th and Harvard), was already transporting two hundred and fifty of his parish children to St. Francis' because St. Thaddeus had no school building. The Sisters of St. Francis assumed the responsibility of riding the city buses with the youngsters. Avalon was predominantly black, and the children being bused were blacks.

A transformation of the area was just beginning. As the whites left, and blacks moved in with their families, the number of children in the parish increased. I can remember Mike's saying, "We never have a funeral in our church."

To work with blacks appeared to Mike to be a wonderful new experience — one which would open new avenues to the apostolate. He proceeded to learn as much as possible about the black culture. Father Patrick Curran, who was already very active in the parish, spent much time with the new curate, acquainting him with the people and with the affairs of the community. Michael was immediately impressed with the warm and friendly congregation. As Father Curran said, "Mike just took the ball and ran with it."

He would spend the rest of his life as a priest in the black community. Unlike many whites, Mike displayed a unique sensitivity coupled with a complete lack of self-consciousness in working with black people. This was a prime factor in his success.

Some years later, my brother's friend, Bob Squires, commented, "Father Dempsey completely adopted the black feelings and life. He was prepared by his very nature for his work." Then Bob added with a smile, "He just had to go through the seminary to get his union card."

Vatican II had convened in October of 1962. By the following spring my brother was serving on the local Liturgical Commission, which, as a result of the Vatican Council's directives, was working out the plans for changes in the Liturgy. This required his attending many outside meetings. The language of the Mass was going to be English, the altars were being turned about, and there was to be more active participation of the lay people in the Mass. All these innovations were of great interest to him.

Surely anyone who knew Mike would agree that in matters of faith and moral principles he was a traditionalist: he accepted Christ's word as the unchangeable standard. At the same time he was recognized by many as a modern "jet set" priest who sought to update the external facets of religion. Indeed, the Mass was the core of his life. If a translation to English would make the Mass more understandable, or if the addition of guitars would appeal to the young, or if the introduction of favorite Protestant hymns would enhance the devotion of the faithful, he considered these changes necessary. His hope as a member of the Liturgical Commission was to increase in the Catholic people the appreciation of the Mass. He thought that the Mass must be so available to them that daily attendance would be an intrinsic part of their lives. The shortening of the fasting time before Communion and the introduction of the evening Mass were big steps in that direction.

He welcomed the new roles of commentator and lector because they brought lay people into the sanctuary. Mike might have remembered the joy of participation, when, as small children, we walked in procession behind the priest who carried the Blessed Sacrament during special services.

The parish community, as we remembered it, no longer existed. The city had grown in population, in boundaries, and in complexity, so that it was impossible for the clergy to reach out to all. Mike saw a real need for reinforcements to come from the ranks of a dedicated laity. It was for this reason that he continued to work with the lay apostolate. Within a relatively few years the ancient order of lay-deacon was restored into the fabric of the Church, and ordained laymen were ministering many priestly services.

During the early 1960s, when Mike would have dinner with

us at home, and we would relax with coffee afterwards, someone would likely ask, "What's new in the Church, Father D?"

Mike would answer with a little smile, "Nothing is really new — just some of the customs of the early Church are coming back."

Father McHugo had appointed Mike chaplain for the parish's Christian Family Movement Society. Many years back, Mike had organized CFM in St. Mary's. At that time, Jack and I, who were long-time members, had interested Mike in the idea of starting a group in his parish and had sent some of our CFM friends to help him run his first meeting.

Each CFM group — and some parishes had several — was comprised of six or seven couples who met regularly in the informal social atmosphere of their homes to study the Scriptures and to plan together a practical application of the Scripture lessons to the issues of the day. The discussion program was structured to focus on family life, as well as to educate and activate the members so that they would be prepared to branch out into various areas of the lay apostolate.

Jack and I were attending a CFM meeting one evening when the discussion happened to be about civil rights. At this time the civil rights issue had gained great recognition throughout the country. Blacks were being heard, and their goal of gaining the human rights to which they were entitled as members of the human race, appeared to be more attainable. Our members felt that they were really concerned, but had no way of communicating their interest in civil rights.

I leaned over to Jack and asked, "Do you think we could work out something with Father D's parish?"

He answered, "Suggest it."

I did. And everyone thought it would be really stimulating to meet with black CFMers.

Michael gladly extended our invitation to the St. Francis' people. When they met at our house, our chaplain, Father Phil Cahill, and our group enthusiastically turned out for the occasion. Someone said, "Won't it be interesting if the neighbors think the Burkes are selling their house to blacks?" This remark was funny only because in the early 1960s that possibly could have caused some kind of panic.

As the guests arrived, our children, who were always our unofficial attendance-takers, did their customary peeking from behind a wall every time the doorbell rang. Earlier that day our son Dick, who had performed the task of setting out the ashtrays, had asked, "Do black people smoke?"

The conversation warmed up quickly. Since we all were family people, we easily found our common denominator. We talked about our children. Then we advanced to neighborhoods and jobs. It was delightful to find that the two races could be so comfortable together. And Mike sat in a big chair, just enjoying it all.

There wasn't a moment's lull in the chatter as we crowded in the dining room for refreshments. Usually our CFM meetings ended after we left the dining room; but this one didn't. Now we were discussing personal racial conflicts. Everyone felt free to make frank comments and to ask questions of the others. I remember Peggy Hatchett saying, "I don't want to be described as colored. I'm black."

Helen Hassett asked, "Is it customary for blacks to be formal? The blacks I know never call me by my first name."

Jean, a black lady, said, "Darlene, you referred to us as 'you people.' Do you consider us a different kind of people?"

The comments were sincere and our openness united us. In the final analysis, everyone agreed that blacks must concentrate on getting the best education possible in order to achieve their rightful place in society.

It must have been after one-thirty in the morning when our gathering broke up, and strangers were parting as friends. And, when the St. Francis' group invited us to visit, so many CFMers attended that the meeting was held in the parish hall.

I especially remember that meeting at St. Francis because the evening was concluded by the joining of hands of all those present, and the singing of the civil rights' movement's theme song, "We Shall Overcome." This was a new and moving experience for us Northsiders.

But, Michael's assignment at St. Francis was to be a relatively short one. After only two and a half years, he was transferred again. All of our family attended the reception which the parish people prepared at the time of his leaving. The tears in the eyes of his friends once more gave evidence of the love that existed between a dedicated priest and the flock to whom he had been assigned.

St. Francis was not only his introduction into the black community, but our family's as well; and it was the beginning of many valued friendships.

When Michael had any news to tell, he phoned each of his three sisters individually. On New Year's Eve in 1964, he gave each of us a call. It was evident from the sound of his voice that we were about to hear something exciting. He began by saying that Cardinal Meyer had summoned him to the Chancery Office that morning. The cardinal had asked him to assume the pastorship of Our Lady of Lourdes Church in the Lawndale area, at Fifteenth Street and Keeler Avenue.

Michael was elated. I'm sure he had been storing ideas all through the years for projects he could undertake if he were in a position to operate on his own initiative. Possibly, during the summer after ordination, when he sat on our front porch with his pen and notebook, he was preparing for this day.

Earlier in the day, after he had left the cardinal's office, Mike had called Father Curran at St. Francis' rectory. The two of them were in the habit of batting jokes back and forth. "Pat, are you sitting down?" Mike asked.

"Okay Mike, let's have it," Father Curran responded.

"Well, I've just been made a pastor," Mike announced.

"Mike, it's New Year's Eve, and you can be pardoned for anything," Father Curran said laughingly. "But that's too big a joke for me to accept. Leave your car where it is, and take a cab home."

Strangely enough, this was probably the last assignment given by our Cardinal Meyer to any of his priests. Very shortly afterwards, the cardinal underwent surgery for a brain tumor, and he never recovered. He remained in a coma until his death the following April.

CHAPTER EIGHT

LOURDES, A CENTER OF ACTIVITY

MICHAEL HAD BEEN requested to move into the new rectory immediately. Therefore he had to pack quickly so that he could be there right after the new year began. When he arrived, he was met by a welcoming committee of parish ladies who had spent the morning getting the rectory in shining order for him. Of course, all of the family appeared almost as soon. Everyone went for a tour of the church, the school, and the rectory.

Although Lourdes was located in a very poor, inner-city neighborhood, in Father D's eyes the parish buildings were castles of worship, of learning, and of living. Such an assignment was surely the culmination of his priestly ambition. He beamed with happiness as he escorted us and told us of his plans and hopes.

The young, genial assistant at the parish was Father Edward Maxa. He "broke in" the new pastor by alerting him to the accomplishments and the needs of the parish.

Father Dempsey was succeeding Father James Cermak at Our Lady of Lourdes. Father Cermak had been a much-loved pastor, and he had many, many projects operating in the parish.

Because Father Cermak was suffering from a serious heart ailment, Cardinal Meyer had offered to relieve him of his duties as pastor. Father Cermak agreed, but only under one condition: he wanted to have a voice in choosing his successor. His projects were very important to the parish, and he wished to be replaced by a pastor who would continue them. (Apparently Father Dempsey, who, at the age of forty-six, was young for a pastorship by Chicago standards, was the man who Father Cermak thought could "fill the bill.")

Before leaving Lourdes, Father Cermak had asked some of his dedicated parishioners to be on hand to offer their continued loyalty when the new pastor should arrive.

Sue and Bill Kirkpatrick decided to give the new priest three days in which to move in and settle down before they would stop in at the rectory to offer their services. They found Father Dempsey sitting alone in his office at dusk, possibly meditating on the tremendous responsibility he was about to undertake. He immediately recognized their names and said, "Oh, you are Bill and this is Sue. Father Cermak has told me all about you."

He had many things to discuss with Bill. First of all he knew that Bill Kirkpatrick was head usher, manager of the credit union, and the one who counted the collection. "Bill," he said, "you are already doing enough. We are going to get a lot of people involved in the work."

Then he went on to ask what societies were already existing in the parish. As Mr. Kirkpatrick mentioned the Holy Name Society, the St. Vincent De Paul Society, etc., Father Dempsey would ask, "Is it good for the people?"

Bill would answer, "Yes, Father. It is good for the people."

The new pastor would say, "Then we'll keep it."

Finally they agreed that, for the present, everything would remain the same.

Mr. Kirkpatrick mentioned that the Knights of St. Peter Claver would be conducting their monthly inner-council meeting on the following Tuesday evening.

The Knights of St. Peter Claver was a Catholic fraternal society for blacks, similar to the Knights of Columbus. This organization was named for a Catalan Jesuit priest who died in 1654, after spending forty years in America, where he devoted himself especially to Negroes.

The former pastor had been chaplain for the Knights, and Bill Kirkpatrick thought that the new pastor might like to attend the meeting.

Father Dempsey did attend the inner-council meeting, and he was completely taken by surprise when Bill nominated him to succeed Father Cermak as chaplain. Mr. Kirkpatrick's suggestion was unanimously accepted, and Father Dempsey suddenly found himself in the honored position of chaplain for the Chicago Inner-Council of the Knights of St. Peter Claver and for the Ladies' Auxiliary.

Dorothy Lewis was the next Lawndale resident to ring the doorbell at the rectory. She said, "Father, I heard that you are in need of a cook, and I will be willing to help you out for two weeks until you find someone."

The new pastor smiled in amazement. "Who told you that?" he asked.

"Rose Bousha, down the block, told me," Dorothy answered.

Michael quickly accepted Dorothy's generous offer. She told me much later that after the first two weeks had passed, she mentioned leaving. "Father Dempsey looked so sad," she said, "and he pleaded, 'Dorothy, don't leave us.'" So Dorothy just stayed on. She was the kind of person who would be quite impossible to replace. Not only did she do an excellent job in the kitchen, but in her charming manner, she extended the hospitality of the house to all.

Although Dorothy was a Catholic, her husband, Reverend Lewis, was a Methodist minister. For years he had conducted Bible classes in their home.

The first project Michael undertook as a pastor was a door-to-door survey of the entire parish. He had printed a questionnaire to be presented to all of the people living in the area, regardless of whether they belonged to the Church. Some of the parishioners promptly volunteered to do the footwork. Charlie Brown and his young son, Mike, were in on the action too.

They canvassed the entire neighborhood, identifying with Our Lady of Lourdes Church and asking: "What do you need? What does the neighborhood need? What can the Church do for you?" People expressed their needs and their ideas willingly and openly.

There was already a very good ecumenical spirit in Lawndale. Father Cermak had met regularly with all the local clergymen. Soon a Protestant congregation purchased new pews for its church, and the neighborly pastor donated to Lourdes the pews that were being discarded. Father Dempsey was very appreciative, as this greatly improved the church. He also considered another change that he would like to make. He thought that the figure of the dying Christ on the crucifix above the altar should be replaced by a figure of the living Christ. He decided that on his next visit with the Hastings he would discuss this with Bill, since Bill had much artistic ability.

Bill Hastings immediately envisioned the picture he would paint and mount, and he proceeded to produce the beautiful, large figure of Christ which still hangs above the altar at Lourdes.

Many of the people who were to be very important in my brother's future life had appeared within the first few days after his arrival at Lourdes.

Monroe Sullivan was one of these. Mr. Sullivan was a young man from Oak Park who was serving on the staff of the Catholic Interracial Council. As the council's assistant director, he was trying to start some kind of practical program which the agency could sponsor.

He had been meeting with Father Cermak in the summer and fall of 1964, discussing a number of ideas, one of which was to start an employment program. When Father Cermak was transferred, Monroe Sullivan was in the midst of drafting a proposal for an employment center, and he regarded Father Cermak's leaving as a real disappointment.

Mr. Sullivan immediately approached Father Dempsey with the proposal and with the suggestion that an employment office might be initially set up in the basement of the rectory.

Father Dempsey listened attentively. Then Mr. Sullivan asked him directly, "What do you think, Father?"

Father Dempsey seemed predisposed to the plan and he needed no convincing. He quickly responded, "Sounds like a good idea. Let's go."

As Bill Kirkpatrick remarked later, "Upon Father Dempsey's saying 'Yes' when he could have said 'No,' depended the whole future of an important program. But then," Bill added, "Father Dempsey never said 'No' to anything that would help people."

By the summer of 1965 the employment agency was taking shape. A section in the back of the school basement, which heretofore had been used as a storage space, was cleared and converted into an office. Across the street, in the rectory basement, typewriters were set up and some office training was available. Monroe Sullivan, who preferred to be called "Moe," was still working on the proposal and running some experimental interviewing in the new office to see if it could really place people.

Father Dempsey was having inserted in the church bulletin printed notices informing people that anyone interested in finding employment could contact this new office. He personally visited nearby factories to ask for job openings. He even went so far as to send representatives into the neighborhood bars and poolrooms to seek out men who were in need of employment. People started coming, and Mr. Sullivan interviewed them.

The late Pat Crowley, who, with his wife Patty, founded the Christian Family Movement in Chicago, turned in the first job orders for a friend who owned a company. Some local people were placed.

The employment office was soon proving itself. A service located in a neighborhood, efficiently run, could reach people and be of assistance to them. The staff, consisting of a few neighborhood people, would place a person in a job. If the person failed, they would help him find another position until he found the place where he was best suited.

The Office of Economic Opportunity had just been established, and a formal proposal was drawn up for this office. Sargent Shriver had been a former president of the Catholic Interracial Council and had been very active in social programs. Now he was the national director of this new economic opportunity program.

It was at this time that Father Dempsey was about to meet his first big challenge as pastor. Mike used this occasion in a very positive way — to advance the new employment program.

There had been an accident in August of 1965 wherein a black woman had been struck and killed by a fire truck which was coming out of its station at Wilcox and Pulaski. When the firemen were responding to a call this woman was standing next to a signpost. The tiller man, in swinging the rig around at the back end, missed his turn and hit the post. It was the sharp signpost that killed her.

This unfortunately triggered new emotions in an already tense situation. The firehouse had recently been picketed by local people because it was not integrated. Now, the black population in the area was ready to flare up in reprisal for the woman's death. The warmth of the evening had brought everyone outdoors.

The accident happened at eight o'clock in the evening. Deputy Police Superintendent Sam Nolan, who was coordinator of the Human Relations Section of the Chicago Police Department at the time, remembers well the course of events. He happened to be in the neighborhood attending a meeting at Crane High School when the call came to Police Headquarters. By ten o'clock, the police were well aware of the seriousness of the problem with which they were dealing. They remained on the scene until four in the morning.

Trouble erupted again the next evening. Father Dempsey went to Wilcox Street with some of the neighborhood ministers and priests to try to calm the people. During the course of the evening, the car in which he was riding was shot at by a youth who was standing in the street.

Father Dempsey, recognizing the fellow and knowing him to be an unstable person who needed help, convinced him to give up the gun. Instead of reporting him to the police, Father Dempsey went to talk to the boy's mother.

Not only the Westside clergymen, but His Honor, Mayor

Richard J. Daley were very concerned. The Mayor asked the local pastors of every denomination to attend a meeting in his City Hall office to confer with him regarding the firehouse incident.

Before attending this meeting, Father Dempsey discussed with Moe Sullivan what he should say to the mayor. He decided to tell the mayor that he had a program to start a service in the community that would really help people. At the meeting he told the mayor that it was these kinds of things that would ultimately solve racial injustice and other problems — not just putting out this fire now and another fire next week. He suggested that coming up with concrete programs was the answer to racial disturbances.

Mayor Daley was very impressed with Father Dempsey. He thought the priest was a good, practical man with a practical idea. Apparently this good impression helped. Two weeks later, the local Office of Economic Opportunity announced that a grant would be given for the employment program. Then Moe Sullivan went to work for Father Dempsey.

The funds came through in September, and on October 1, 1965, the employment center known as Lawndale for Better Jobs opened its doors in the basement of Lourdes' school. A large sign bearing the official name was tacked onto the building. This occasion might have been reminiscent of the day in 1935 when Mike tacked the telegram, which was Dad's call to work, onto our living room wall.

Monroe Sullivan was the director of Lawndale, and Jack Robinson was his assistant. Emma Tulley, Virginia Easterly, Loretta Douden, Helen Appleton, and Catherine Arnold, all of whom were local women, were on the staff.

This was a dedicated crew with goals to achieve. First, the office must become known; people must be interviewed and sent out on jobs; and the score sheet for jobs found must show good results. There was much enthusiasm and much hard work involved. The program was being funded for a three-month period, and it could survive only on success.

Happily, by January, the records showed that there had been as many as ten placements a week. The future of the program looked promising. It was obviously becoming known in the community. People were coming in and being placed in jobs.

Now the staff began investigating the basic problems in discrimination. Mr. Sullivan met with an Equal Employment Opportunity official from one of the government offices and talked about the need for ending discrimination in the trucking industry. He felt that community people were being excluded from jobs for only one reason — they were black.

When the funding from the Office of Economic Opportunity was extended for another six months, it was indeed a relief to the staff of Lawndale for Better Jobs.

Moe Sullivan knew Gene Callahan, who was the executive director of the Chicago Conference on Religion and Race, an ecumenical social agency.

The agency had been formed some years previously when a nationwide meeting had been held in Chicago for the purpose of establishing such a conference in each large city. The basic thrust was to unite the efforts of the various religions in working out the problems involving race, housing, employment, etc.

Our city was the one in which the plan got "off the ground" most successfully. Cardinal Meyer was credited for this because of his ability to sit down and work with his counterparts. The cardinal had appointed Mike's classmate, Monsignor John Egan, who was pastor of Presentation parish in Lawndale, and Father Edward Egan as the archdiocesan representatives to this conference.

Since Father Dempsey was known to be interested in ecumenical work, Monroe Sullivan arranged for him to meet with Gene Callahan. At a breakfast meeting with Mr. Callahan, Father Dempsey, the Reverend Robert Christ (who later became head of the Chicago presbyter of the Presbyterian Church), Robert Squires, a member of the conference staff, Robert LeFlore, Monroe Sullivan, and a few others, there was a discussion about what to do with the employment program in Lawndale. Since it appeared to be very successful, they discussed the possibility of expanding to other neighborhoods and getting other religions involved in sponsoring it. This seemed very logical.

They agreed to work out an expanded concept for a city-wide program which would involve the Protestant, Jewish, and Catholic faiths.

In May of 1966, they met again. This meeting was held in Father Dempsey's study, a tiny room adjoining his equally small bedroom; it housed his wall-to-wall collection of books. Now they had a proposal for an expanded concept, and they needed a new name — one that would encompass the three faiths that were expected to sponsor the program. The name "Tri-Faith" was suggested by Gene Callahan and approved by all.

The Conference on Religion and Race would be the umbrella covering the new Tri-Faith employment program. Indeed, sponsoring this kind of social action was the purpose for which the conference had been founded.

From there, representatives of the group, including the Reverend Christ, Gene Callahan, Robert Squires, Jack Robinson, and Al Hanley, who was a member of the diocesan poverty office, went to Washington to do the "politicking."

Roman Pucinski, a Congressman from the Eleventh District, was one of their key contacts in Washington. He "opened doors" for them. They met with Sargent Shriver. Mr. Shriver thought it was a good idea, and soon the mayor's office funded the program.

When a press conference was held for the purpose of announcing the new city-wide employment project, our new archbishop, John P. Cody, was present, in one of his first public appearances in our city. Archbishop Cody had been appointed to head the Chicago Archdiocese in August; he had been Bishop of New Orleans. Father Dempsey, who was known to prefer working behind the scenes, was not at the press conference. However, when his name was mentioned, the archbishop seemed to be already familiar with his work.

Soon an advisory committee, which was to be the governing body for the expanded Tri-Faith program, was formed, and Father Dempsey became its chairman.

Then Monroe Sullivan left Lawndale and went downtown to operate the new program from the 116 South Michigan Avenue office of the Conference on Religion and Race. Jack Robinson assumed the directorship of the local Lawndale Tri-Faith office.

Jack Robinson and his staff operated the employment office very successfully. Eventually Mr. Robinson also left Lawndale and went to work in the Human Relations Department of the Archdiocese of Boston. In turn, he was succeeded by Robert LeFlore, and then, Emma Tulley. Mr. LeFlore recalls, "It was very gratifying to know that Father Dempsey invested complete confidence in me. Father Dempsey might not go into the office for a week or two because he knew that the staff was working efficiently." After Robert LeFlore was promoted and transferred, Emma Tulley became the director until her death a year and a half later. Then Michael's first-found friend, Bill Kirkpatrick, who had left a job that he had held for fifteen years in order to become Mrs. Tulley's assistant, became the director of the employment office. He is still in charge of this office.

Tri-Faith was a tremendous success story. The office placed more than three hundred persons in its first year of operation. An enormous amount of work had been done by a staff of neighborhood people who had to produce quickly in order to be re-funded regularly.

Offices were opened in seven locations throughout the city. Six and a half years later, ninety-two thousand, four hundred and sixty-five placements had been made. Interesting to note, is the fact that one of these offices was in Michael's former neighborhood, Uptown.

At the present, though most of the original crew have left, the substantial program which they initiated, still flourishes.

Lourdes was a center of activity, not only for the people of the parish, but also for the Westside, and in a sense, the entire city — and the Church in the United States. Father Dempsey and the lay people he worked with were the vanguard of a newfound Church involvement in social issues. His record here no doubt was the reason he was tapped for the Campaign for Human Development in later years.

While a section of the Lourdes' school basement was being transferred into a busy employment office, new plans were being made in the school itself. As was typical of Father Dempsey, he had quickly made friends with the children, whom he fondly called "my kids." He wanted only the best for them.

When Bishop William McManus, the superintendent of the Archdiocesan Catholic Schools, called a group of pastors to attend a meeting, Michael was among those invited. The purpose of the meeting was to plan a program for busing inner-city school children to schools outside of their neighborhoods where it appeared that they would have educational advantages.

Father Charles Langan, the pastor of Divine Infant parish in suburban Westchester, was also present at this meeting, and he was one of the pastors who expressed a willingness to participate in the program. Lourdes and Divine Infant were located in the same geographical direction; and therefore, they were teamed for the busing. Then Father Langan and Michael were expected to work out the plans. Each met with his own school board and the parents whose children would be involved in order to explain the program and to receive approval. Father Dempsey spoke in Westchester too.

His great love for his parishioners was so evident that his concern for them was contagious.

As a result of the parish meetings, it was arranged that the black families would continue paying tuition at Lourdes so as not to take needed revenue from the school; and Divine Infant would enroll the students tuition-free.

Then Mike went out shopping for a used bus. He was not only happy to be able to purchase a bus, but also to find that Rose Wess, a mother who wanted a job, was willing to assume the responsibility of daily driving the children. The transportation was subsidized by the Archdiocesan School Board. The office of Father Edward Egan, co-chancellor for Human Relations and Ecumenism, was responsible for the initial work on the busing program.

This Westchester parish was an affluent one; but its greatest asset was the generosity of its people. Father Langan was rightfully proud of them.

Thirty-two Lourdes' children arrived in the yellow bus on the first day. They found Father Langan, the whole faculty, and the eighth-grade students waiting outside the school to greet them.

Soon the parish mothers were inviting the black youngsters to come for lunch. The Westchester parents and their pastor visited with the new students' parents at Lourdes. "It was a noble effort, and it worked out mutually well," Father Langan said. "I'm glad we did it."

Unfortunately, the bus proved to be not in the best condition, and keeping it in running order was frequently a frustration. Dorothy remembers, "Rose would get way out there and she'd call me and say, 'Dorothy, tell 'em I'm stuck again.' "

Integrating the Westchester school was very harmoniously achieved because it had been so well-planned. However, only about nine or ten parishes in the whole archdiocese attempted a similar busing program.

At the same time the busing of public school children caused great racial conflict, not only in Chicago but in cities throughout the nation. For this reason, some of Lourdes' parents had been reluctant to send their youngsters out of their neighborhood until the program had been tried.

Through Father Dempsey's efforts, many children, after graduation from Divine Infant, went on to Westchester's Immaculate Heart of Mary High School for Girls and St. Joseph's High

School for Boys.

Mike's first year at Lourdes had been one of great involvement; but he was destined for a much greater involvement.

CHAPTER NINE

LAWNDALE AND BEYOND

ARCHBISHOP CODY WAS noticing Father Dempsey's abilities and leadership qualities. In January of 1966 he gave Mike the first of many special assignments. The archbishop asked Mike to plan and host a testimonial dinner for the newly-consecrated Bishop Harold Perry of New Orleans. Bishop Perry, a former Chicagoan, was the first black in modern times to serve in the hierarchy of the Catholic Church in the United States. Like Father Dempsey, he was a chaplain for the Knights of St. Peter Claver.

Mike immediately called upon the Knights and Ladies. They worked diligently with him to accomplish the splendid celebration which took place downtown in the Pick-Congress Hotel. Our talented brother-in-law, Bill Hastings, painted the copy of Bishop Perry's coat-of-arms which hung above the speaker's table. The guest of honor was delighted by his hometown welcome, and a generous sum was raised to aid him in his Inner-City Apostolate in the South.

On occasions such as this, Michael was always very happy to have us with him. We would remain in the background because we knew he had so many people to greet; but he would find us and introduce us to everyone he chatted with along the way. Thus we had the pleasure of meeting many wonderful people.

The Knights of St. Peter Claver were proud of their Chicago chaplain. They knew the work he was doing. That summer when they held a convention in New Orleans, they invited Father Dempsey to be present to accept an award medal.

Agnes and Charlie went to the airport to see him off. Agnes happened to meet James Armstrong, who was an officer in the Northern Trust Company, where she too was employed. Mr. Armstrong was taking the same flight. Agnes introduced him to Michael, but as the two boarded the plane, they were separated.

Since Mr. Armstrong had already arranged to rent a car in New Orleans, he decided to wait for the priest to get off the plane and offer him a ride to his destination. Mr. Armstrong stood near the ramp to wait.

Father Dempsey was among the last passengers to leave the plane, and, as he stepped out into view, suddenly a band started playing. It was an escort of Knights in uniform who had come to welcome the Chicago chaplain.

Mike had only a few hours to spend; so he went to the cathedral and received his medal from the Knights' District Deputy, John Woodford, and then returned back home. He always appreciated any kindnesses so much that he would never refuse an invitation regardless of the distance involved.

In the fall of 1966, a new category of archdiocesan offices stemmed from The Second Vatican Council's decree on the pastoral responsibilities of bishops. Vatican II had described a diocese as "a portion of the people of God which is entrusted to a bishop to be shepherded by him with the cooperation of the presbytery."

The Archdiocese of Chicago would be divided into seven administrative units which would be called vicariates. They would include the four hundred and sixty parishes in Cook and Lake counties. The aim of this grouping was to provide a spirit of cooperation in handling the many challenges facing the archdiocese because of changing areas. Formerly white city parishes were now black; and the Church had greatly expanded with the suburban development. Each region was to be headed by a vicar delegate who would hold a one-year appointment and would be eligible for reappointment.

This was soon to mean an important assignment for my brother. Archbishop Cody appointed him to the office of Vicar Delegate of Region IV. For some time before the appointments were announced, the plan had been under consideration.

Each vicar delegate would work from his own pastorate. Therefore, the Lawndale area was Michael's field; but the eighty-two parishes included in his vicariate extended far into the west suburbs.

All of the auxiliary bishops were given the additional title of vicar general. They worked in specific phases of the vicariate programs. (After Michael became a bishop, the Inner-City Apostolate, which included areas far outside of Lawndale, was under his guidance as a vicar general.) All would share with Archbishop Cody the administration of the archdiocese, the largest in the United States, which included two million Catholics.

There was much communication involved in organizing a vicariate so that the needs of each parish would be known; and each vicar delegate made personal visits to the parishes in his territory. He would meet with the priests to discuss pastoral problems, organizational programs, and other matters which would be of great concern to the archbishop. Goal-setting, both spiritual and material, was given great importance. It was planned to have priests working in each region on educational problems, youth, lay activity, etc.

In a letter to the priests of his vicariate, Father Dempsey wrote: "The vicariate structure was established in our archdiocese to help fulfill the pastoral mission of the Church to our people. But the vitality and effectiveness of any structure depend upon the human elements which comprise it.

"The challenges which the vicariate offers to us as priests are boundless. The response we make to them is part of the creative growth essential to the Church's mission. If the vicariate is to be truly effective for the entire community of God's people, then we as priests must respond with creative leadership."

In another letter which he sent to the pastors of his vicariate, he wrote, "Our black Catholic laity is truly the pride of the Church. Their generous commitment to the concerns of the Church has made possible the vital Catholic communities that serve the archdiocese so very well.

"Lay participation is the goal of our times. New creative ministries in the Church are multiplying our hands and our feet, so that our own pastoral ministry is becoming more effective."

My brother was steadily moving up the ecclesiastical ladder. On January 8, 1967, he was elevated to the rank of a domestic prelate and invested in the robes of his new office of monsignor by Archbishop Cody. The investiture service at Lourdes was beautiful and impressive. Michael's friend and classmate, Monsignor Jack Egan, preached the homily. All the parishioners attended with the same joy and pride that we, his family, experienced. Our Father D looked very elegant in his new red vestments. This was the first time we saw him walk up the aisle of the church flanked by an honor guard of the Knights of St. Peter Claver, who, in their full uniforms, added great dignity to the occasion.

Everyone proceeded from the church to the Driftwood Restaurant for dinner. The new monsignor, preferring to have the attention focused on others, and being aware of the fact that this was the seventh birthday of his niece, Mary Angela Brown, gave her a special introduction, and asked the guests to sing "Happy Birthday" to her.

Then he called upon Uncle Bob Ryan, who was eighty-nine and the only remaining member of our older generation. Bob's tear-filled eyes expressed his joy when he greeted Michael's friends.

Just a week later, Lourdes' parish was to experience another memorable day. Vice President Hubert Humphrey had notified Monsignor Dempsey that he would be in our city on January 17, and that he would like to visit at Lourdes to see the federally-funded programs in action.

Indeed it was a big event when the Vice President, accompanied by Mayor Richard Daly and other dignitaries, and escorted by our Archbishop John Cody, arrived in limousines on South Keeler Avenue. It was very encouraging to know that the Vice President had an interest in the many programs for the poor that were being tested in this inner-city neighborhood.

Included in their tour was a visit to the school lunch room where two hundred and thirty students benefited from a federally-funded lunch program. There were many smiling faces in that lunch room as the pastor introduced his young friends to the "hand-shaking" dignitaries.

However, Humphrey's visit to Chicago did not reach the front page of the newspapers because McCormick Place had been destroyed by fire on the preceding night. The fire at the exhibit hall was the front-page news.

In June of that year, Archbishop Cody went to Rome, where Pope Paul VI bestowed the "red hat" upon him. The cardinal-elect, thinking that Mike was in need of a brief vacation, invited my brother to accompany him for the ceremonies. Mike Dempsey had never dreamed of seeing Rome. Much less had he anticipated ever being present for an occasion such as this. He greatly enjoyed these few days, but his heart ever remained in Lawndale.

In October, John Cardinal Cody appointed Mike the co-ordinator of all inner-city work of the Roman Catholic Archdiocese of Chicago. This was a major appointment. Michael would be brought into a supervisory relationship with many archdiocesan agencies which, until now, had been operating with relative autonomy. He was given an office upstairs of a Walgreen's Drug Store at Cicero and Madison. This was about a mile and a half from his rectory. It was called the Westside Chancery. From this office he would coordinate the inner-city affairs. He hired Elaine Williams as his secretary.

Michael was also to serve as liaison with federal and municipal administrations on redevelopment projects which would affect Catholic parishes and institutions in urban renewal areas. He was to continue as pastor of Our Lady of Lourdes. One of his parishioners told us that every time the pastor received another responsibility, the people were afraid that possibly it might mean that he would be taken from the parish.

Then a lady added, "But he promised that he would never leave us."

Monsignor Dempsey's response to the newsmen who questioned him regarding his new appointment as inner-city coordinator was: "It is not a matter of authority, but of leadership. I am to coordinate the activities of the archdiocesan agencies and not in the least restrict what they are doing, but coordinate for better communication between the many church groups working in the inner-city so that they have a greater potential to work in the same general direction.

"The priests in the inner-city have been asking for years that someone assume leadership for better communication among agencies all working for the same goal."

Cardinal Cody set up a steering committee to help Michael. On this board were representatives of many archdiocesan agencies. Their duty was to keep the various organizations aware of what other groups were doing. This would avoid any conflict of effort or duplication of services in the work of the various organizations.

Five years later, when my brother was asked by a reporter about the Inner-City Apostolate, Mike replied: "It is something the Church must have. We are in a changing situation. Over a period of a couple of years, the need of the Church to be a relevant sign to a changing community makes the assessment of parish priorities a continually new dialogue for priests and people. It is my task to go in and help priests and people adjust to a changing city.

"Cardinal Cody had the vision to see that the archdiocese could not relate to the many minority groups of the Church as though they had no relationship to one another. In the archdiocese we are one Church. Hence there is one apostolate, not many.

"It is part of the process of being Church to help Latin-American people to have concern for their black friends who are poor, and to help the blacks to see the human need of other cultures in the one Church. Then the whole Church works together to form the Body of Christ. The entire archdiocese, rich and poor alike, have so much to share in faith and trust, sacrifice and wholehearted giving."

And, at the time that Michael was assigned to the Apostolate, late in 1967, Cardinal Cody, along with Father Edward Egan, his delegate to the Conference on Religion and Race, was approaching John Baird of the Baird and Warner Real Estate about his firm's interest in low-income housing for inner-city residents. Baird and Warner was a major Chicago real estate firm.

Mr. Baird was one of the few lay members of the Conference on Religion and Race. He had originally joined the board as a favor to Monsignor Jack Egan, who had been helpful to him on the Metropolitan Housing and Planning Council. Mr. Baird had developed a deep interest in the affairs of the Conference and was most eager to help in the field of housing. Elzie Higginbottom of Baird and Warner immediately joined John Baird in this endeavor.

This was prior to the 1968 Housing Act. They planned to utilize Section 236 of the Federal Housing Authority Act, which provided for financing the kind of housing that appeared feasible. Their recommendation was that the limited dividend approach was better than the non-profit.

Monsignor Dempsey was very anxious to have a building project erected in his Lawndale community, and he was willing to do anything he could to accomplish this. He volunteered to help the realtors find investors. His method was to go into a wealthy suburban parish and first "sell" the pastor on the idea of investing in the poor. Then he would set up an appointment, at which time the realtors would meet with a group of parishioners whom the pastor had contacted and who would be prospective investors. This was the way in which the initial funds were raised.

The investors then worked with Interaction, a non-denominational group of black and white businessmen who were willing and able to help any community group in the building of two hundred and thirty-six housing units. The Baird and Warner people then sought a suitable location for the buildings.

CHAPTER TEN

THE TURBULENT SIXTIES

WITH CIVIL RIGHTS as the theme of the decade, the 1960s were a time of critical racial unrest throughout the United States. Out of Atlanta, the Reverend Martin Luther King, Jr. emerged as a great black leader, renowned and respected as the author of non-violent demonstrations. He led protest marches in large cities throughout the nation, as blacks continued to strive for equal rights.

Dr. King made only one serious attempt at bringing the cause to the North. Chicago was his target. He called it the most segregated city in the North. In January of 1966, Dr. King and the SCLC (Southern Christian Leadership Council) staff arrived in Chicago to lay the groundwork for the Chicago movement.

That summer Dr. King moved his family into a dilapidated Lawndale apartment in the 1500 block of South Hamlin Avenue. He took up residency in Chicago in an effort to focus attention on ghetto living conditions, while at the same time he was preparing for the giant rally which was to take place July 10 in Soldier Field. The day of the rally was to be known as "Freedom Sunday."

Fifty thousand people attended the Chicago rally. They cheered as Reverend King read his demands — a massive, detailed program to bring about racial justice in the city. From there he led a march to City Hall to present the demands to Mayor Daly. Of course, City Hall was closed on Sunday, and Dr. King nailed his demands onto the closed door of the building. The march was a non-violent demonstration which appeared to evoke good will from the predominantly black bystanders and participants.

The next morning Dr. King and his associates met with Mayor Daly to discuss their demands. The mayor turned them down. Almost as soon as the mayor's rejection was publicized, outbreaks of violence erupted in some neighborhoods, including Lawndale. Shots were heard along Fifteenth Street. Dr. King sent his wife, Coretta, and their four children back to Atlanta, but the minister remained in the city to concentrate the Chicago movement on open housing. He met with tremendous opposition from white homeowners when he led a march into a suburban community.

Soon after, in an effort to calm the impending storm, a conference was held. At this time the staff of the Chicago Conference on Religion and Race brought Dr. King and the city authorities together. Although an agreement on open housing was reached, it was generally felt that the agreement was never satisfactorily implemented. Dr. King was not successful in Chicago.

On April 4, 1968, the great black leader lay dead in Memphis — the victim of an assassin's bullet. I don't think my brother ever met Dr. King; but on the following Tuesday, April 9, he flew to Atlanta to attend the funeral, and returned immediately after. Along with tens of thousands who could not fit into the Ebenezer Baptist Church, he listened outside in the broiling sunshine to the funeral services that were transmitted to the crowd over loudspeakers.

News of the shooting sent shock waves throughout the entire country. Chicago — and the Westside — was no exception. By noon of the following day, rioting had begun. The disturbance on the Westside of Chicago originated when classes were dismissed at Marshall High School at Kedzie and Adams; and the trouble mushroomed.

Lourdes' School closed at noon and some of the Sisters and priests stood outside as the parents came to take their children home. Calls kept coming into the rectory. One mother, who was working downtown, was in hysterics when she phoned. She had heard that the whole city of Chicago was being blown up. She screamed, "My baby is in Lourdes and they're burning up the city."

Things were really happening. By one o'clock in the afternoon, all of the Lourdes' priests were in front of the rectory looking south down Keeler Avenue. The local excitement was taking place two blocks away at Mason School, which was one of the largest public schools in the city. Mason had closed too, and the children coming along the street, were greeting the priests. Blue helmets could be seen in the distance as police officers quickly moved about. Young people could be seen rocking squad cars back and forth until the cars turned over and rested upside down like dying beetles.

Just a mile and a half north, at Madison and Kildare, the priests at St. Mel's were standing on the roof of their rectory. They could see a crowd coming down from Marshall. Among the young people were two of Mike's rough friends from the high school who had joined just for a lark.

By Saturday afternoon, the staff at Lourdes decided to put up a bunting. One of the Sisters dyed a bed sheet a deep purple color. Father Purtell contacted his classmate, Father Earl Thomas, who was a photographer, and asked him for some pictures of Dr. King. One of the priests centered a picture on the purple sheet and tacked it outside of the church. Other pictures were tacked onto the school and the rectory. It was fortunate that Father Thomas had provided about twenty-five copies, because many neighbors came by to ask for pictures.

That night, just as the sun went down, the fires started. Fathers Tom Purtell and Henry Pehler, Bob Melcher, a deacon who was serving at the parish, and Michael, watched from the second-floor windows. Father Tom said, "It was just like Nuremberg — the glowing of fire on Pulaski Road — an orange light glowing."

Then Mike called Ed Street, a parishioner who lived on Komensky, and asked, "What's goin' on, Ed? It looks like the sparks and flames will catch you."

Ed answered, "No. It's on the east side of Pulaski, Father; but the fire department is there now."

"It was eerie," according to Father Tom. "The fire department had to respond to the calls, but in order not to alarm the people, the firemen didn't turn on the sirens. It was like watching a silent movie. The big hook-and-ladders would come 'round the corners without a sound."

The next day, April 6, the neighborhood was calm, but the stores along Madison Street and down Roosevelt Road were ruthlessly set aflame. They were ransacked and looted before being burned out.

At Lourdes' rectory crank calls were coming in from outside the neighborhood. Whites were saying, "What's a matter with you people? You should shoot everybody."

Cardinal Cody was in constant communication with Michael on the phone. They decided to set up a place where people who were burned out could get food and clothing. Both Washington Boulevard Methodist Episcopal and St. Catherine of Sienna churches offered the use of their parish halls for the collection. The churches were located across the street from one another at Washington and Austin, in Oak Park; and this became the headquarters.

The cardinal said, "Michael, we'll give Our Lady of Lourdes' phone number to the media." Consequently, the radio and television newsmen were announcing that anyone wishing to donate food or clothing should either bring it to one of the Oak Park churches or call the Cardinal's Committee at Lourdes' number. The Lourdes' priests took turns answering the calls. When they picked up the phone, instead of saying "Our Lady of Lourdes," they said, "Cardinal's Committee." The phone rang constantly.

Father Purtell, answering one phone call, heard, "This is Cardinal Cody. I'm heading out to the Westside now. What's the best way to go?"

Father Purtell cautioned, "Your Eminence, I'd like to tell you that from what I've heard, it's best to stay off the Eisenhower. They are throwing rocks and bottles from the overpasses." Disregarding the warning, the cardinal went right on to Lourdes.

Hate calls came through too on the publicized line. In one of these calls, which Mike received, a fellow said, "I have something I'd like to donate for black people if they can use them."

Father Dempsey asked, "What is it?"

"Six grave lots," the man answered as he banged the receiver down.

The Cardinal's Committee planned that the neighborhood people would distribute the food right from Lourdes' school yard, the psychology being that the white absentee landlords should not be giving the alms. Abraham and Marceline Rideau and a crew of parish people issued food from the open doors of the priests' garage adjoining the school yard. Long lines of people had gathered there. Most of the folks who were burned out lived above stores along the business streets. Their apartments, of course, were destroyed with the stores. Each was asked, "How many people are in your family?" Then they were given the ration of canned goods already packed for that number. No one was questioned as to whether he really needed it; everyone was served quickly and pleasantly.

Great amounts of food were stacked in the school yard. Big milk trucks and bread delivery trucks were arriving, and their drivers were dropping off the entire load.

Because of the nature of the riots, it was amazing to blacks that white people were taking it upon themselves to be so generous. Many thought it was because of Father Dempsey. People wanted to help him.

All the Lourdes' priests were out, even late at night, walking the streets as far as Roosevelt Road. They were urging parents to keep their children indoors. The natural curiosity of children made it difficult to shelter them. "Everyone was worried for the priests," Marceline Rideau recalls. "But the priests weren't concerned at all for themselves."

On one of these mornings, when Bill Kirkpatrick was on his way to work in the employment office, he observed Father Dempsey circling the block on foot, apparently checking to see if the neighborhood was as peaceful as it appeared to be at that hour. Bill became frightened, and he shouted, "Father, what are you doing outside?"

Michael calmly answered, "I'm taking my morning walk, Bill."

Bill told me later, "We were just worried to death about him. No white person would be alive if he walked through the streets of Lawndale during the riots. But, no one ever hurt him. It was the kids — they had brought the word throughout the neighborhood that he was their friend. Everyone knew that; and everyone knew what he was doing too. No one would touch him."

Of course, the family was very concerned. My sisters and I made calls to the rectory. Mike pacified us by minimizing the situation and assuring us that everything would be all right; and that he was in no danger.

Father Purtell had occasion to see a little humor in the scene when a three-year-old girl came clattering along Keeler Avenue. She was sporting the fanciest kind of spangled cowboy boots, which appeared to be about a size nine. Berger's Shoe Store had indeed been looted.

Surely the residents of Lawndale will never forget the day when the National Guard arrived. By that time, the Westside had been officially declared a disaster area. All day long the big Army trucks circled the neighborhood. The soldiers, armed with guns, sat grimly scanning all within view of their slowly-moving trucks. It was like a war-torn city; and no one was smiling.

I know that my brother understood how anger and desperation could drive people to react in the way that they did; but it deeply saddened him to see it happen. He knew that the great numbers who participated in the riots were so few, when compared with the peaceful majority who had already endured so much, and who now had even more to suffer.

It took about a week before peace was restored. But the

shopping districts, where most of the damage was done, were not rebuilt to their former states. Many merchants never returned to business in that area. Even to this day, the local people are experiencing the loss that resulted from destruction. They still have the inconvenience of having to go out of their neighborhood to shop.

CHAPTER ELEVEN

A JOYOUS INTERLUDE

EARLY IN MAY of 1968, a week after the twenty-fifth anniversary of Father D's ordination, he made one of his early morning "catch you while you're still at home" calls to each of us three sisters. He began by saying, "I have some news for you." He hesitated and then went on, "How would you like to have a bishop in the family?"

I replied with a startled "Father D, what are you telling me? Are you going to be a bishop?"

I'm sure Kay and Agnes must have given much the same response. After I had calmed down somewhat, he went on to say that he had just received the appointment from Rome and that it was doubly exciting because his friend and classmate, Alfred Abramowicz, was also to become a bishop. Cardinal Cody would consecrate them together, and the date for consecration would be decided shortly.

By the time the joyous news was announced publicly, we were at the height of elation. Our friends called excitedly to express their happiness and good wishes.

The newspapers printed John Cardinal Cody's statement: "The announcement by the Apostolic Delegate, Archbishop Luigi Raimondi, that the Holy Father, Pope Paul VI, has assigned two new auxiliary bishops for the Archdiocese of Chicago, will bring joy and satisfaction to the priests of the archdiocese.

"I welcome these two zealous priests, Monsignor Dempsey and Monsignor Abramowicz, to assist me in the tremendous task of administering the affairs of the largest archdiocese in our country. Both have demonstrated their priestly zeal, their pastoral ability, and their dedication to service in the tasks that have been assigned to them.

"I am indeed most grateful to the Holy Father and I am honored too, by the confidence which he has placed in these two Chicago priests by their appointment as members of the Catholic Hierarchy of the United States."

Father D suggested that Agnes, Kay, and I meet with him to compile a list of people to be invited to the ceremony, as well as to plan the festivities. We chose a Sunday evening, and met at Browns' home in Schaumburg. Our cousin, Agnes Ryan, was there too, and she commented that it was good to see the four of us working together so happily, away from the big family. Michael's only regret was that the number of guests had to be limited; he wanted to invite everyone.

He and Bishop-elect Abramowicz had selected Quigley Seminary South for the place of consecration and for the dinner which would follow. This seminary was much newer than their alma mater, Quigley North, and a beautiful building, indeed. The chapel was very large and modern in design; and the simplicity of a gymnasium setting for the banquet would surely harmonize with the natures of the two men.

June 13th, the Feast of Corpus Christi, was the day of consecration, and it was a day of days for all who had any part in it. How privileged we were!

I recalled that at the time of Michael's ordination in 1943, Mother, being a sentimentalist, had given each of us girls an extra copy of his invitation to be kept for the fine husband she hoped each would find in the future. She wanted her then unknown sons-in-law to be included in the happiness of that great day. Mom never even thought of the possibility that Jack, Charlie, and Bill would all be present for this, Michael's second ordination.

For his coat of arms, our brother selected figures from the arms of the Dempsey family in the upper right of the shield, and from the Ryan family in the lower left.

These were the Irish Dempsey arms consisting of a silver lion erect between two swords against a red background. As befit a bishop, the swords were converted to a crozier, or shepherd's staff. The Ryan family arms displayed a griffin's head, shown between a pair of angel wings to honor Michael's baptismal patron, St. Michael the Archangel. Dividing the shield diagonally was a gold band bearing two hands clasped in friendship and love, an expression of Michael's pastoral efforts to bring about ecumenical and interracial unity in metropolitan Chicago.

The motto "Deus Meus Adjutor Meus" (derived from the Seventh Psalm: "My God, my help") was chosen by him to honor Samuel Cardinal Stritch. The wording was identical to the motto of Cardinal Stritch, who had ordained Michael to the priesthood.

The external ornaments of the arms were a professional cross and a green broad-brimmed hat with six tassels on either side. The tasseled hat was the clerical counterpart in heraldry to the layman's military helmet. Together with the cross it indicated the office of bishop.

The sun shone in all its glory that warm afternoon; and, in our estimation, the world couldn't have appeared more beautiful. The Abramowicz and Dempsey families, dressed in their new finery, congregated in the foyer outside the entrance to the Sacred Heart Chapel. Then all proceeded to the front seats which were reserved for the two families. The chapel was comfortably air-cooled in contrast to the ninety-degree temperature outdoors. Soft music and fragrant flowers helped to create a beautiful atmosphere.

Then the processional began. The Church in all its glory, in all its tradition, in its unity, in its strength, and in its ecumenism was portrayed as the continuous stream of hierarchy and clergy of all faiths, in splendid vestments, walked to their assigned positions.

Lastly, the two classmates, Alfred Abramowicz and Michael Dempsey, attired in pure white vestments, and giving the impression of being humbly uneasy, followed, and took their respective places in the sacristy.

The ceremony was lengthy, as John Cardinal Cody, in this most solemn rite of the Church, consecrated his two new auxiliaries. The Offertory gifts were brought to the altar by members of the families and by friends who resided in the bishops' parishes.

At the conclusion of the beautiful and symbolic service, the bishops arose, each wearing the miter which signified leadership; the episcopal ring, which was a gift from the cardinal and symbolized the bishop's marriage to his flock; and the pectoral cross which was a sign of his faith in Christ. Each held a crozier which signified that he was a shepherd.

Then, the joyful and triumphant tone of the trumpets penetrated the walls as though all heaven opened, as the recessional began; and once more the Church in all its splendor walked through the aisle. Our brother Michael and his life-time friend Alfred, were bishops!

At the banquet which followed in Quigley's gymnasium, the guests spent some enjoyable hours greeting one another in this happy atmosphere. The band, being very obliging, merrily played the favorite Polish and Irish melodies. The memories of this day will forever be our treasure.

Our brother, the bishop, didn't want anyone to miss the rejoicing. Realizing that many of our cousins who were present at the consecration had tickets only for the adults in their families, he planned a second celebration on the following evening, for all of the young people.

The festivities were held in St. Viator's, which was the parish we Burkes attended. Our pastor, Father Eugene Sullivan, was honored to accommodate the new bishop with the parish facilities.

St. Viator's chapel was a cozy scene for a family Mass. The servers, the commentators, the musicians, and the vocalist were all part of our young "home talent." Everyone joined hands as we circled around the altar at the Consecration of the Mass. The season's graduates were mentioned by name, and we prayed for their success.

Because of the greatness of the occasion, Agnes, Kay, and I were permitted for the first time to receive the Holy Eucharist under both Species.

After Mass we moved to the lounge in St. Viator's school, which soon resounded with the noise and excitement of the large crowd of youngsters.

Father Phil Cahill had been toastmaster at the banquet which followed Father D's first Mass in 1943, and he happily assumed the duties of toastmaster again.

His opening remark was, "There is an old saying, 'Be kind to the office boy because he might be your boss some day.'" Then he went on to say that his first meeting with Bishop Dempsey was at the time the Dempsey family moved into St. Sylvester's parish, and Michael, who was then a seminarian, came into the rectory to introduce himself. Father Cahill continued, "I answered the doorbell and I treated him nicely."

After a few speakers had added their words of congratulations, the toastmaster announced that the young people had prepared some special entertainment. Father Cahill had even rehearsed them himself.

When Marge Kane stepped to the piano and began playing the Notre Dame Cheer Song, all the youngsters arose from their tables and marched onto the stage, loudly singing the new words which I had written to the melody of the Notre Dame song — words which expressed the love and appreciation of all the nieces and nephews, and all the "cousins' cousins," for their own dear Father D.

Ordination,
May 1, 1943

First Blessing of
Mother and Father,
May 1, 1943

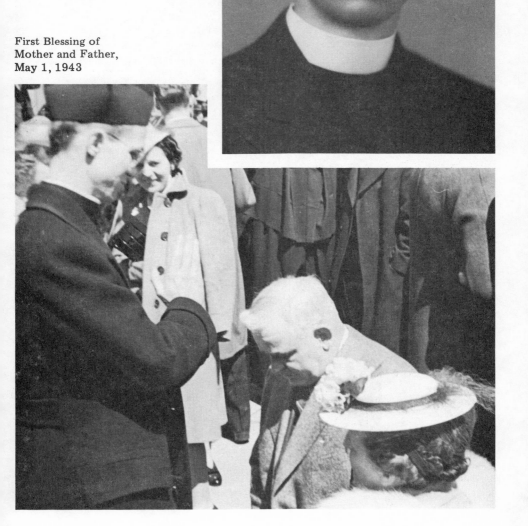

LAWNDALE FOR BETTER JOBS

" A Neighborhood Employment Center "

1449 So. Keeler   Phone 277-8700

IN COOPERATION WITH THE

LAWNDALE   URBAN   PROGRESS   CENTER
3140 W. ROOSEVELT RD.

ENTER AT ALLEY ON 15ᵀᴴ ST.

"If a man has a job, most of his other problems can be solved," said Bishop Dempsey (r) as he discusses the job problem with his associates, Monroe Sullivan (l), Bob Squires, and Mrs. Emma Tully.

Vice President Hubert Humphrey meets with Bishop Dempsey and community leaders in the Lawndale For Better Jobs office in January, 1967.

February, 1966 Fund-Raising Dinner for newly-consecrated Bishop Harold Perry of New Orleans. Bishop Perry is in the center. He is flanked by John Cardinal Cody of Chicago, and John Woodford, District Deputy of the Knights of St. Peter Claver.

The Family

(Above) Edward Dempsey with Agnes, Michael and Ann — 1925.

(Right) Dempsey's Christmas Card sent out in 1921 [Ann and Michael].

(Below) Visiting Sunday at Seminary, 1938. Ann, Mother, Kay, Grandfather, Michael, Dad and Agnes.

Mike, third from left, with classmates doing Seminary chores.

Michael on stage in Seminary play.

Barrett 2746 Fullerton Ave., Chicago.

Bishops Mother at age 17.

Dempsey, the Bishop's Mother at age 17.

Grandmother Ryan's house on Logan Blvd.

On the Campaign Tour

(Above) The Fourth Annual Meeting of the Diocesan Bureau of Human Relations Services, Augusta, Maine, October 22, 1971. From left to right: the Most Reverend Peter L. Gerety, D.D., Bishop of Portland, Maine; the Honorable Kenneth M. Curtis, Governor of Maine; the Most Reverend Edward C. O'Leary, D.D., Auxiliary Bishop; the Most Reverend Michael R. Dempsey, D.D.; Mr. Neil D. Michaud, Diocesan Director, Diocesan Bureau of Human Relations Services.

(Right) on the tour — Bishop Dempsey, Bishop Edmond McCarthy of Maine and Jim Prior.

His Kids

(Left) Bishop Dempsey surrounded by his young friends in Lawndale. He knew them by their first names and they looked forward to his visits.

(Bottom) Bishop Dempsey takes time out of jam-packed schedule to umpire a neighborhood game for his kids.

(Above) Eskimo children are one of the groups of people helped by the Campaign for Human Development through self-help grants.

(Left) Decent housing with water sewers and electricity is desperately needed by thousands of hard-working Indians in the United States. The Campaign for Human Development, of which Bishop Dempsey was the first National Director, is trying to solve this problem.

(Both NC Photos)

Bishop Michael Ryan Dempsey had many exceptional qualities and one of his natural talents was listening.

Funeral Mass for Bishop Dempsey at Our Lady of Lourdes' Church, Chicago, January 9, 1974.

Cheer, cheer, for
*   Our Father D.*
Now you have joined
*   The hierarchy.*
We're all proud to say that we
*   Belong to a bishop's family.*

You've been our uncle
*   So many years;*
Tied up our shoestrings,
*   Wiped off our tears.*
We're all proud to say that we
*   Belong to a bishop's family.*

You've taken us to picnics,
*   Museums and parks;*
Checked on our report cards,
*   Tipped us for good marks.*
We're all proud to say that we
*   Belong to a bishop's family.*

All through the years you've
*   Followed us along.*
Now as you see,
*   We're all big and strong.*
We're all proud to say that we
*   Belong to a bishop's family.*

Now we'll hear a cheer from   (Hastings cheer)
*   All the Hastings crowd.*
Wouldn't you believe it,
*   Browns are just as loud!*   (Browns cheer)
Now the Burkes will join in too;   (Burkes cheer)
*   And all our cheers are just for you.*

Sure, we'll hear from Kanes   (Kanes & Jacobs cheer)
*   And the Jacobs now.*
And we'll bring up Father D;
*   He can take a bow.*   (Youngest children escort
We're all proud to say that we   him to stage)
*   Belong to a bishop's family.*

Cheer, cheer, for
    Our Father D.   (All swinging clasped hands)
Now you'll be called
    "Your Excellency";
But at home you'll always be,
    None other than our Father D.

Now we'll call on everyone
    In this hall to stand.   (All rise)
Wouldn't you say this evening's
    Been just really grand?
Let's all give a great big cheer;   (All cheer)
God bless our Father D.

Needless to say, Father D was truly thrilled by this surprise tribute. He was then presented with a copy of the song, which had been autographed by all who were present.

On Sunday, Michael offered a pontifical Mass at Our Lady of Lourdes. This was followed by a banquet which the Ladies of St. Peter Claver hosted at the Driftwood Restaurant. This too was a fine affair and a joy to all who participated.

One memory of the day is especially precious. After leaving the dinner at the Driftwood, we drove back to the rectory with Michael. A large crowd of children was waiting outside for him to return. They were suddenly all calling him "Bishop" and asking him to autograph the souvenir parish bulletins which they had received at Mass that morning. They hung on to his arms and escorted him to his door. From then on he was "Bishop" to all the children at Lourdes.

There was still another day of celebration before the years of hard work that ensued. Michael was invited back to St. Francis De Paula the following week. His former parishioners had prepared a joyous celebration. There too the trumpets blared as the pontifical Mass began.

CHAPTER TWELVE

HIS EXCELLENCY, THE PARISH PRIEST

THE HAPPY AND exciting days of celebration soon ended, and Bishop Dempsey was back in the full swing of activity.

Soon some people were speculating: "Dempsey will get a big plush parish now." But those people should have guessed that Mike, in accepting the office of bishop, had asked the cardinal to let him remain at Our Lady of Lourdes. The parish people knew he wouldn't leave; and the honor that accompanied his appointment to the hierarchy brought honor to the Lourdes' parish family.

By nature Michael was a typical small-town priest. I think that this was the image to which he aspired during his seminary days and that it had developed from his earliest memories of the parish priests he knew at St. Francis Xavier's Church.

Now, as a bishop, he intended to continue doing as much parish work as possible. He still gave family instructions in the faith, and he wanted to keep all of his personal contacts with his parishioners. In later years he said, "Of all the functions a bishop is called upon to perform in his episcopal ministry, I don't think there is anything that is more satisfying, more gratifying, than those he performs as a pastor, as shepherd."

And so it was that even though his boundaries and his responsibilities, as well as his authority and his contacts, expanded, Mike Dempsey remained the same man; and the rectory at Our Lady of Lourdes reflected his personality.

One of the advantages of his remaining in Lawndale was that he was right there where the problems were. He would ask of others, "Why are these things happening? How can I help?" If he didn't know, he would not rest until he found the answers — and that was the "name of the game." He would pray, research, and then act with confidence.

Father Maxa had been transferred shortly after Michael's assignment to Lourdes. Then, by the fall of 1967, when Mike had become involved in so many outside activities, Cardinal Cody appointed Father Henry Pehler administrator of the parish. He and Father Purtell were very dedicated and hard-working, and were greatly appreciated by the parish people. Like the pastor, the associate priests were always on the friendliest of terms with the neighborhood children.

For two years, as coordinator of the inner-city affairs of the archdiocese, Mike had been going into his office on Cicero Avenue every day. Now he decided that it would be more convenient for him to operate the office from his rectory. Elaine Williams had done an excellent job in the Office of the Inner-City Apostolate, but she was no longer able to continue. Mike was in need of a secretary. He looked over his parish for another person who would really care about the inner-city projects, and he decided to ask Virginia Easterly to change jobs. She was willing.

Virginia was a neighborhood woman who worked in the Tri-Faith Employment Office across the street from Lourdes. She was a convert to the faith. Virginia was a big woman, and she had a heart to match. She continued to thrust her whole heart into the affairs of the Church in Lawndale. In future years she extended her untiring efforts to the cause of the Campaign for Human Development. Virginia, like Dorothy Lewis, contributed much to the efficiency and the pleasant atmosphere of the rectory.

Among the dedicated people at Lourdes were the Benedictine Sisters from Lisle, Illinois, who staffed the school. Their activities extended far beyond the classrooms as they worked diligently with the parents in many educational programs for the young, not only during the school year but in summer as well.

The Sisters went to great effort in planning the Liturgy and music for their early morning Masses in the convent chapel. The priest who celebrated the Mass especially enjoyed being a part of the beautiful ceremony which always gave a new day a great beginning.

Sister Joanne Form, the young, vivacious principal with a charming Texas accent, trained a choir consisting of a lively group of children who transmitted their enthusiasm for music to all who heard them perform. Added to this group were the talented teenagers who comprised a combo. Their drums, accompanying the loud singing and the rhythmic clapping of the grade-school choir, could be heard blocks away. Mike was truly proud of them.

It was our family's custom to attend Lourdes' midnight Mass on Christmas Eve. Members of other priests' families would be there also. Hearing this kind of music in church was an experience for us, because it was so completely different from the music in our traditional Mass at home.

Dorothy always expected us to come, and she would leave sandwiches and a pot of coffee on the dining room table before she finished her day's work.

This Westside neighborhood was a turbulent one; its crime rate was high, the use of narcotics was prevalent, and life was cheap. My brother suffered much because of his keen awareness of these conditions. When he asked, "Why are these things happening? How can I help?" he was indeed weeping inside. He saw people suffering and people being mistreated.

But a most concerned and loving people also resided in Lawndale. These were the people Mike spoke about later when he traveled the country seeking understanding and help for the poor. "The poor don't even know they are poor. They think they are rich when they start counting their blessings. They are not only rich in the things that really matter, but they help to enrich others by their noble outlook on life."

He was then presenting a movie about the life of the poor. "We call our movie *The Land of the Brave*. The greatest bravery in America today is the bravery it takes to live in the world of the poor without any hope, unless someone else unlocks the door to let you out."

Dorothy Lewis still recalls some occasions when, as the rectory housekeeper, she would be responsible for greeting many kinds of people. "The bishop would be afraid for me when I'd turn those drinkin' folks away. I'd even threaten to call the police to some of them. Then he would be worried 'bout me."

" 'Oh, Dorothy! Don't do that,' he'd say.

"And I'd answer, 'Listen Bishop, I'm not afraid of them.' And then he would want to take me home—that couple of blocks. He'd want to bring me home. I'd say, 'No, Bishop, you just take some rest. They're not gonna bother me.'

"I went back one morning and he told me, 'Dorothy, I followed you home last night.' But I wasn't afraid. I was only afraid for him. I didn't want him to be out on the streets. They wasn't gonna bother me; I always carried my walkin' stick 'cause my feet would be so tired."

But, "Bishop Dempsey saw only two kinds of people," in the words of Bill Kirkpatrick, "the well-off and the poor. He wanted to help the poor. He didn't see color or religion or age; he didn't question whether a person was good or bad. Anyone who was poor was welcome to his friendship and his services."

There were times when Mike's extending his friendship brought him into situations unlike what might be expected in a priest's life. On one occasion, a fellow named Red had taken part in a gambling game on Sixteenth Street. In the course of events he had shot and killed a police officer. As Red was running from the scene of the shooting, he told some of his companions that he would only "turn himself in" to Bishop Dempsey.

The police, being unaware of the fleeing man's intentions, had sent out a city-wide alert.

Soon Red arrived at the door of Lourdes' rectory. Bishop Dempsey, answering the doorbell, found the man, who was about thirty-five years old, trembling, and with the gun still in his hand.

The bishop brought him into the house; and the six-foot-five fugitive towered above the pastor. In his kind and patient manner, Bishop Dempsey prevailed upon his distraught friend to report himself to the authorities; but, seeing that the fellow was not yet willing, my brother invited him to stay for the night, with the promise of accompanying him, as soon as Red could muster up the courage to bring himself to the police.

On the following day they appeared together on the Court-house stairs, where the officers took Red into custody.

And there were times when Bishop Dempsey was called upon to defend the rights of his young people. In one instance, a couple, who were his friends, was planning to be married. It happened that the young lady's Southside parish had no church building. Services were held in the school. She approached her parish priest, the one who would perform the ceremony, about finding her a church for the wedding. The priest took her out in his car to look over several churches in the area.

She selected a nearby, beautiful, and newly-built suburban church. The pastor of the neighboring church was cordial, but he felt that it was not yet the time for blacks to be married in a white parish.

When the bride-to-be told her fiance about her disappointment in not being able to obtain the church of her choice for the wedding, the young man decided to call Bishop Dempsey and ask his advice. The bishop was obviously concerned, and he said, "I'll call you back."

Then Bishop Dempsey very diplomatically made a phone call to the suburban pastor. In his usual friendly way, he said that he would be in that parish on a particular Saturday to offer the Mass at the wedding of his friends.

On the day of the wedding a large crowd of white people

gathered on the corners opposite the church. They had come out of curiosity to see the black couple being married.

Another example of Michael's interest in other people's lives occurred when he heard that an FBI agent and his wife were adopting another child. They had already adopted four white children, and this was their second black child.

After seeking advice from their friends about the prospects of happily raising a bi-racial family in a suburban location, they had decided that giving the children much love would be the most important consideration; and this was the deciding factor.

Bishop Dempsey had met the Boyles at one time, and he wanted to go out to Mt. Prospect to attend the baptism of the little boy. However, confirmations filled his schedule so that he had only a little time to spare, and that would be late in the day; but he still drove out, though it was quite a distance to Mt. Prospect, to personally extend his good wishes to this family.

One of the things that made Bishop Dempsey an amazing person was that although he had a very methodical mind, he scheduled his day in such a way as to include everyone, and it might have appeared that he had no priorities. At breakfast one of the priests would ask, "What do you have on for today, Mike?"

The bishop would answer something like, "Well, I'm going to fix that window on the second floor of the school now." Somewhere through the years after becoming a pastor, Mike had acquired a great amount of know-how from his "Do-It-Yourself" books. "Then there's a committee meeting downtown at eleven. I'll come back home after that because I want to repair that faucet in the basement before I go to the diocesan consultants' meeting. Then I'll take the kids out for hamburgers."

Other mornings after breakfast, Mike remained at the table until he had read all the letters written to him by the children he had confirmed on the previous evening. He made a habit of sending notepaper to the school where confirmation was scheduled, with a request that every child write him a letter stating the reasons why he or she wished to receive the sacrament. When Mike reminded the priest accompanying him to the confirmation, "Don't forget to bring home the letters," his smile indicated how much he enjoyed them.

No doubt Bishop Dempsey was unaware of his influence in the life of a lady who happened to be shopping in a community discount store one Saturday morning. Although her children were

Catholics, she was not a member of the Church. When she observed the bishop in the store, pushing a shopping cart and filling it with clothing for the three children who accompanied him, she decided to join his Church.

And Marceline Rideau remembers calling the bishop one night. Her neighbor's house had just been the target of a fire bomb. Marceline only wanted Michael's advice about where to get help. Not only did he call in the Red Cross, but he was there himself presently to see what he could do for these people whom he had never met before.

Soon after he became a bishop, Michael had been assigned by Cardinal Cody to the board of the Conference on Religion and Race. At that time housing was the immediate concern of the Conference. A year earlier, Michael had helped the realtors to find people who were willing to invest in low-income housing. Mike had long been distressed by the fact that very many of his fine neighbors were living in the shabbiest of houses, and he knew that Baird and Warner were ready to build in the area if a proper site were available.

It happened that the Coca-Cola Company owned some land in Lawndale, at Eighteenth Street and Kostner Avenue. The realtors had approached Coca-Cola in regard to acquiring this site, but their offer was rejected on the grounds that the company definitely wanted to keep the property.

Gene Callahan tells the story of how my brother arranged to have himself invited to a bishops' meeting in Atlanta, Georgia. This afforded him an opportunity to be in that city and to drop in casually at the national headquarters of the Coca-Cola Company. The bishop introduced himself and stated his business. He convinced the officials that the property in Lawndale would not be a good site for their plant.

They agreed that if an adequate or better location could be found, that they would trade the Eighteenth Street land. Soon afterwards a trade was made. Based on Bishop Dempsey's arguments, some Church property appeared to be more suitable to the company's needs. The land in Lawndale was purchased, and in 1969 construction began on Lawndale Manor.

John Baird jokingly told the bishop, "If you ever have to leave the Church, Bishop, you have a job in the real estate business."

During these years there was much picketing and vandalism

on construction sites. Everywhere, including the University of Illinois, construction was stopped for this reason. Heretofore, McCormick Place was the only site where the builders were able to continue with their work. Now, the operation in Lawndale proceeded without incident. Baird and Warner attributed the uninterrupted progress of their building on Eighteenth Street to the influence in the community of the bishop and the members of his parish.

Throughout the construction period, Michael was very active in referring the initial tenants. The realtors gave Lourdes' people preference, in that they had the first opportunity to lease. Bishop Dempsey also referred other people who might not be members, but who had gone to the parish to seek help in finding housing. He personally counseled prospective tenants who had any kind of problem.

By November of 1970, the lovely two-story yellow brick buildings, comprising two hundred and thirty-five modern apartments, were completed. Lawndale Manor was ready for occupancy.

CHAPTER THIRTEEN

"MY KIDS"

NO ACCOUNT OF Michael Dempsey's life would be complete without telling the important role the children played. Every child in Lawndale might have considered himself or herself a special friend of the bishop; and that was the way Mike wanted it. Throughout his lifetime he retained the magnetism which had attracted children to him in his youthful days.

After assuming the pastorship of Lourdes, Mike, in making the schedules, allotted himself Saturday as his regular day off. He chose that day because he wanted to spend his free day with the children.

In springtime a young and energetic crew of youngsters eagerly waited for him after six-thirty Mass on Saturday mornings. They immediately began working in the large yard in back of the rectory or in the small garden at the front. Sometimes when Father Purtell was preparing for the eight-thirty Mass, he would hear water running and think that a rain had started; and then he'd realize that what he heard was the sound of the backyard sprinklers, an indication that the children were already working.

The children enjoyed digging and fertilizing and planting the lawn and the flowers. Then, during the summer, they kept the grass well-trimmed. Surely all who passed by appreciated the beautiful results of their efforts. From my earliest memories of my brother, I can recall that he was exhilarated by the fragrance of the spring air and the feel of the fresh black soil.

Being a natural outdoorsman, he always kept his fishing poles in the trunk of his car — just in case an opportunity would arise — and he delighted in sharing the magic of the open road with the children. His friends, the Nickersons, owned a cottage near Benton Harbor which he was welcome to use. Then he had a few other favorite places to take the youngsters for an overnight trip.

At one time Mike formed a Boy Scout troop. Soon the troop was making plans for a great weekend in the outdoors. Some fathers were going along too. The fellows were to spend the afternoon at Fort Dearborn, have dinner there, and enjoy the next day with activities. But they arrived only to find that a tornado was heading toward the area, and reluctantly the whole group turned back home.

Years before, Father Curran had dubbed Mike the "eternal optimist" because Mike never frowned; everything would be all right. This was one of those occasions. So Mike promised the boys that they would go out again the following weekend, and they did.

The next attempt was a grand success. Some of the youngsters had never seen horses before, other than on the television screen, and meeting a horse face to face was a real thrill. On the night that the boys returned, Father Purtell was anxiously waiting to hear the account of their expedition. They enthusiastically related their experiences. "Father, that horse got a big ol' eye. I never seen a big ol' eye like that," one child said excitedly.

Another Scout brought back a frog. The boy was very happy to have a new pet, and he kept the frog at home in the bath tub. Every time Father Purtell saw Leroy, he asked, "How's the frog doing?"

One day when he asked, Leroy answered, "Aw Father, it's gone. A rat ate it."

It happened that a fellow who was writing a story on the inner-city was staying at Lourdes. His wife was a musician and a folk singer. When she heard about the frog's sad fate, she was so moved that she wrote a song about Leroy and the frog.

In the parish, everything was geared to the children. The priests never restricted their friendship to those who attended Lourdes' School. The students who attended Hughes and Mason came to the pastor with their report cards too. The rectory was always open to them. The youngsters were welcome to go upstairs to Father Dempsey's study, where they could find an assortment of puzzles which he had for their use. These were tricky finger puzzles with numbers. Mike considered them educational.

My brother also kept a little lending library. A few shelves of his own collection had children's books mixed in; and the incongruity was quite amusing. Next to a tall book printed in Latin might be the *Life of Willie Mays*. The children really enjoyed using the pastor's personal library and they were proud to tell him how many books they had read.

Mike especially had a watchful eye for any children who were nonconformists. Marion and Jerry, who lived down the block, near Fourteenth, were among those in this category. The brothers were good boys and they were very intelligent, but they just didn't like to go to school.

Sometimes, when Michael would be leaving the rectory in the morning, he would happen to notice Marion and Jerry outside playing ball. When they would see him they knew that they were in trouble. They would run behind big trees in their attempt to hide from the pastor. On one occasion Jerry dashed for home, and Mike, knowing that their mother was away at work, decided to take over the situation himself. He followed directly behind the lad and up the back stairs. Soon Jerry was getting into Father Dempsey's car and he was taken right into Hughes School. The fellows quickly learned that the pastor had no tolerance for nonsense.

The neighborhood children affectionately called him "Bishop" as they had done on the day of his first pontifical Mass at the parish. They had a real appreciation of the fact that a bishop belonged to them.

One little boy made a habit of ringing the doorbell of the rectory as many as eight times in a day. When someone pushed the buzzer to let him in, this little fellow would enter, saying slowly, "Bish-shop, Bish-shop."

If he heard one of the priests telling him, "Dear, he's not home," the child would silently close the door; but he would keep coming back until he found the bishop at home.

Bill Kirkpatrick called Michael the "Pied Piper." Bill said, "I could look down the street and there wouldn't be a child in sight. Then the bishop would come along and they seemed to come up out of the sidewalks, all wanting to hang on to his arms."

Even if he were on his way to attend a wake, Mike would fill his car with the children who came to greet him. They probably anticipated a stop at McDonald's on the way home. One lady told me that the people in the parking lot at McDonald's found it amusing to see an unbelievable number of children coming out of a Ford Torino. "It was like a television commercial for small cars," she said. As each child stepped out, the bishop handed him or her a dollar to spend.

It was always an exciting day for Michael and the young people when Deputy Superintendent Sam Nolan and some of the other police officers came to Lawndale. The men would bring a supply of basketballs, softballs, bats, and other sporting goods for the children.

The deputy said, "Bishop Dempsey got the biggest kick out of it because this was used as a wedge to open the doors of misunderstanding between some police officers and the kids out there. It would break the ice — the barrier. The bishop would be even happier than the kids because he could see a good rapport developing between the law enforcement personnel and the young people."

Bill Kirkpatrick tells this story about his meeting Mike unexpectedly on the street one winter morning. Bill had driven Sue to work. It was still dark at six-thirty when he passed along Fourteenth Street and recognized the pastor's car parked at a curb. Bill wondered what Bishop Dempsey would be doing there at that time of the morning. As he approached more closely, he observed that many people were quickly moving about inside the car. His first thought was that a gang was beating up the bishop. Bill's instant reaction was to park and rescue his friend.

Just then, the door of the bishop's car opened, and as the light went on inside, Bill could see that the active crowd in the car was Lourdes' own high school students who were daily bused to St. Joseph's in Westchester. The school bus had broken down again, and the bishop was making the rounds, gathering all of them, which meant his making more than one trip to Westchester. Obviously he considered school attendance very important.

Knowing the importance the pastor placed on attendance, a student who missed the bus would feel free to go to the rectory and ask one of the priests for a ride; and they came frequently.

Michael strongly urged families to give their children a Catholic education; but many families were unable to pay the ever-increasing cost of tuition in the Catholic high schools. Mike would only have to look back to his own schooldays to appreciate their problem. Now as a bishop, he was in a position to seek help for "his kids," and to be successful in obtaining scholarships to various schools. Because of his interest in education, he knew personally the principals of most of the high schools.

At one time Gordon Tech gave him six scholarships. Mike thought he should share the good fortune, so he kept only three, and gave the remainder to Holy Angels' boys.

The Christian Brothers offered scholarships to their schools too, and the amount granted would be indicated by the needs of a particular family.

Then Mike had still another means by which to help his people in the education of their young. Since it was customary for a pastor to make a donation to any bishop who came to his parish to administer the sacrament of confirmation, Michael was on the receiving end of these financial gifts. The fact that he was the inner-city bishop sometimes motivated the parish people to be even more generous. Mike, in turn, used this money to send many of his young friends through high school.

Lourdes' parishioners were hard-working, family people. It took the salaries of both parents to keep a family going. On one occasion, Michael offered three hundred dollars to "help with school" to a couple who had a large number of children to educate. He explained that someone had given him the money. These parents refused his gift, not because they couldn't use it, but because they could "make it" on their own and they knew that he would easily find another family that needed it more.

Bishop Dempsey also made outside contacts to help talented young students. He was instrumental in getting one young man into West Point, and in helping another Southsider, who later became an officer in Annapolis.

My brother was especially proud of his own Lourdes' students who came back to Lawndale to teach, or to give valuable services in the community programs.

In his office, under the sheet of glass which covered his desk, Michael had crowded together a magnificent collection of pictures of "his kids." The pictures were taken at first Communions, confirmations, and graduations, and they were personally autographed by his young friends. Many snapshots of new babies were sent to him by couples at whose marriages he had officiated.

Soon Bishop Dempsey's devotion to the poor and his effectiveness as their advocate would cause him to be offered the opportunity to go nationwide as head of the Catholic bishops' new campaign.

CHAPTER FOURTEEN

THE BISHOPS RESPOND, AND
MIKE IS CHOSEN

IN THE LATE 1960s appeals were being made to the Catholic bishops for direct social action by the Church to help eradicate the causes of domestic poverty.

Many denominations were getting involved in social action. Mike had been following with great interest the programs of IFCO (Inter-religious Foundation for Community Organization), which was a new style of mission in the life of Christians. IFCO, head-quartered in New York, was a result of a coalition of church organizations that had joined with a number of non-church organizations to create a foundation which functioned independently of the member organizations. It made decisions about the allocation of church resources to support self-determining efforts or community organizing efforts among the minority poor in American society.

Although the Church had always been involved in helping the poor, a nationwide effort by the Catholic Church was a revolutionary idea — a reflection of changes taking place — changes my brother believed in. I'm sure Mike's heart leaped with joy when, at the November, 1969, meeting of the Catholic Bishops of America, in Washington, D.C., a resolution was approved calling for the appointment of an ad hoc committee to develop a plan for a "Bishops' Crusade Against Poverty." John Cardinal Dearden of Detroit, Michigan, President of the NCCB (National Council of Catholic Bishops), appointed the Most Reverend Francis J. Muga-vero, Bishop of Brooklyn, to be chairman of the committee.

When the bishops met in San Francisco the following April, there were two hundred and eighty-four in attendance. At this time it was decided that because of, and in spite of, acute inflation, a sliding economy, and the highest level of joblessness in seven years, the Church could ill afford to wait longer; the national effort must begin in 1970. A proposal was advanced by the Most Reverend Philip M. Hannan, Archbishop of New Orleans, to "raise funds to fight poverty through a special collection to be launched in the Thanksgiving season."

The resolution carried, and the bishops mandated the USCC (United States Catholic Conference), the action arm of the NCCB, to develop a plan to achieve the first national collection in the Catholic Church in the United States aimed at combatting the causes of domestic poverty.

Soon a committee was designated by the Most Reverend Joseph L. Bernardin, general secretary of the NCCB and the USCC, to draw up a plan to include structure, staffing, timetable, and budget estimates for the "Crusade." This committee included Robert B. Beusse, the director of the Department of Communications of the USCC. Their report called for the immediate retention of an executive director and set forth criteria for the position.

As a result of the committee's search and deliberation, the Most Reverend Michael R. Dempsey, auxiliary to the Archbishop of Chicago, was asked to direct the campaign. The committee considered the appointment a stroke of inspired leadership. The guiding presence of a credible, well-informed bishop who had given his life to the poor, was to be the single most important reason for the ultimate success of the campaign.

Cardinal Cody told us later that before accepting the appointment, Michael first asked him for approval. The cardinal said, "Mike, I'm only afraid that the work will kill you." But knowing that his auxiliary wanted more than anything in the world to serve the poor, the cardinal consented.

Robert Beusse agreed to undertake the communications aspect of the new crusade. The role he was to play was essentially that of quarterback. He was to create the grand design for the campaign and act as a catalyst, drawing into the vortex of the campaign the enormous creative energies of all who were to ally themselves to the cause. Timothy Collins immediately became a full-time assistant, and even to this day is planning the fund-raising trips.

The title, Campaign for Human Development, was selected because it would firmly identify the bishops' crusade with the Papal encyclical "Populorum Progressio."

A Papal statement providing the stimulus for the campaign's slogan: "For God's sake . . . break the hellish circle of poverty," was emphasized in all the promotional materials. It was a quote from Pope Paul VI, in his message to French social action workers: "Let all Christians stand in the first rank of those who dare, by every means at their disposal, to break the hellish circle of poverty."

This slogan would express the anguish of the Church over the growing problem of poverty that entrapped succeeding generations. It would sound a clarion call to all Christians to make every effort to eliminate the causes of poverty.

Pope Paul VI had written in his 1967 Encyclical *On The Progress of Peoples*, "No one may appropriate surplus goods solely for his own private use when others lack the bare necessities of life. In short, as the Fathers of the Church and eminent theologians tell us, the right of private property may never be exercised to the detriment of the common good."

The campaign was to have two phases: The first was educational, to dispel society's myths about the poor and their needs. The Educational Component had as its objective the education of Catholics through a two-fold approach: providing information about poverty, social conflict, and human development; and presenting new ways to eliminate the causes of poverty. The second phase was to provide resources, called "self-help" funds, to the poor "for their use as they would see fit."

A Promotional and Public Education Component would deal with the promotional aspects of the campaign and with the education of the general public. Radio and television public service spot announcements would be released carrying the message of the campaign and they would be designed to create and to stimulate awareness of poverty and human development in the listener and the viewer. They would acquaint the old and the young with the virulent dimensions of poverty.

The films and the spot announcements would not be post-scripted. Rather, film and audio would serve as a vehicle to convey the actual voices and faces of the poor to television viewers and radio listeners, so that the audience would experience first-hand what it was that the poor had to say about themselves and about poverty.

Because the National Catholic Office for Radio and Television did not have a broadcast distribution office, Mr. Beusse arranged with the Reverend William Fore, the director of Broadcasting and Film Commission of the National Council of Churches, to employ the Commission's distribution and promotion department, headed by Lois Anderson. This would make possible the dissemination of broadcast and film materials through both Protestant affiliates and Catholic diocesan communications' personnel throughout the nation, and the development of a collaborative network of communications people at the local level to further the support of the campaign program. This was truly an ecumenical alliance.

Such cooperation was made easier by the fact that for years my brother had been known and respected in Protestant circles. As a member of the Archdiocesan Commission on Human Relations and Ecumenism, he had frequently traveled downstate to meet with members of various denominations in an attempt to clarify and strengthen the common bond of faith.

It was planned that organizational meetings would be arranged in various large cities throughout the country. Mr. Beusse contacted Joseph McSweeny, who was the director of Development for the Archdiocese of New Orleans, and asked him to join the campaign staff. Mr. McSweeny took a leave from his work and went to Washington, where he set about organizing a national network of campaign directors.

Mr. McSweeny made a preliminary survey of key dioceses and archdioceses before deciding upon the six cities where the regional meetings would be held. Then he scheduled each city for an October meeting. It was Mr. McSweeny who would lead the task force on its cross-country tour to these regional meetings. Included in his crew was a group that would make presentations designed to activate leaders.

Suzanne Grescoviak joined the task force at Mr. Beusse's invitation. She served as administrative assistant to Mr. McSweeney and therefore provided administrative support for the task force in the months that followed.

Also involved in the development side of the campaign was John Cosgrove, the director of the USCC's Department of Social Development. He provided much of the input of the factual information on the nature and extent of poverty in America.

In addition, Mr. Cosgrove developed the campaign's policy-making structure, application procedures, eligibility and funding criteria, and undertook the enormous task of screening candidates from across the country for the forty-member Nationwide Committee for Human Development.

There were many departments, divisions, offices, and secretariats of the NCCB and the USCC that would be making significant contributions to the campaign.

Mr. Beusse asked James Prior, a journalist and public relations man, to join the task force which would put together the fund-raising and communications aspects of the campaign. One of their first responsibilities was to meet with the newly-appointed national director. James Prior said that heretofore he had met very few bishops. "I didn't know much about what bishops did or how they lived. So it was with some awe that I prepared for my flight to Chicago to meet with Bishop Dempsey," he recalled.

He and Bob Beusse arrived in Chicago on a bright sunny day in August, just a few short months before the date of the first collection. Neither of the men was familiar with Chicago. They took a cab from O'Hare Airport to the bishop's neighborhood. The cabbie found Lawndale, but he didn't know the exact location of Our Lady of Lourdes, and he couldn't find South Keeler Avenue; so he let them off in the general vicinity. As the men walked along, very aware of the fact that they were lost, they agreed that this was one of the worst ghettos they had ever seen. They passed one apartment house that was literally on fire. The people in the house were so accustomed to fires that they didn't even leave the building, but looked out through the windows, watching the fire and waiting for the firemen to come. The streets where the children were playing were filled with garbage.

After roaming some blocks, the two visitors were rescued by policemen cruising in a squad car. The officers suggested that the men call the bishop from the police station. "Our first conversation with Bishop Dempsey," Mr. Prior said, "occurred when we phoned him and admitted to him that we had struck out on finding his rectory. We asked him for more explicit directions. Bishop Dempsey did better than that. He said that he would be right over, and he picked up his frustrated communications experts from New York in the police station. My awe of bishops was beginning to be relieved.

"Bishop Dempsey drove us around the area in his compact black sedan and gave us an even better feel for the lifestyle of the ghetto. I remember thinking to myself how valuable this man was going to be to the Catholic Church's anti-poverty campaign. It was becoming more and more obvious that the national director of the Campaign for Human Development had really paid his dues in the Chicago ghettos.

"We went to Our Lady of Lourdes and talked with him for quite a while. He was a soft-spoken Irishman with a perpetual smile, especially when he talked, and made you know that you were his friend. He told us about the city's high-rise housing developments, where the black mothers couldn't let their children out to play because of the crime on the streets below.

"That night at dinner we had a leisurely conversation about the campaign, and his outlook for it. He was very positive about it, even though it was a new venture for the Church. He gave us confidence and courage — the sign of a true leader of men. He spoke about the campaign as if its success were already assured. I felt that here was a man who had been given a mission by the Church to create something that Christ wanted, that the Campaign for Human Development would help the poor in great and small ways, and that there was simply to be no faltering or turning back. We would succeed because Christ wanted us to succeed."

Robert Beusse immediately began to use all his expertise to make Mike the spokesman for the poor — one who would be effective in dealing with the radio, the television, and the newspapers. Although Michael was extremely well-versed in the problems of the poor and in his recommended solutions to make inroads on poverty, he readily admitted that he had never appeared on radio or television before in his life, nor had he any press conference experience.

To give the bishop some basic training for the press and media encounters awaiting him, Mr. Beusse set up a training day in New York. Bishop Dempsey spent half a day at WOR Radio to practice taping radio interviews, including his responses to very difficult questions posed to him by members of the task force.

In the afternoon of the same day, Michael journeyed to Dunwoodie, New York, to the Archdiocesan Television Center and was given practical on-camera experience in the handling of a television interview.

November 22, 1970, the Sunday before Thanksgiving, was the day set for the collection. It was decided during early September, that the best public relations approach to the Campaign for Human Development would be to program a hard-hitting, nonstop seven-week schedule, not unlike a political campaign or the "blitzing" techniques of a new product introduction in the marketing field.

The USCC's Department of Communications became the headquarters for the campaign. Its offices in New York and Washington were literally taken over for the duration, and both office complexes began to look like political campaign headquarters with stockpiles of literature, strategy maps of campaign regions and other signs of feverish, deadline-oriented activity.

The campaign was to be formally announced at a national press conference on October 1st. The next question was where that conference should be held: Washington, New York, or where?

For a variety of reasons, it was decided to launch the campaign in Chicago, the hometown of Bishop Michael Dempsey. It was further felt that in the short days remaining until the national collection, the spokesman for the campaign had to be firmly established.

Bob Beusse and Jim Prior met with Father James Roache, the information director for the Archdiocese of Chicago, to help plan the press conference. Father Roache was invaluable in his knowledge of and sensitivity to the press in Chicago.

It was important to prepare swiftly for the conference and for the series of regional meetings that would immediately follow that announcement.

Mr. Prior made an advance trip throughout the six-city area to establish local contacts with the press and to prepare the press for the regional visit that would follow.

Similarly, the promotional and educational facets of the campaign were in high gear, and a good deal of material was being written and generated to fall into place at the right time in support of the campaign.

"It was a new idea and the task force who worked on it did so with a certain all-out urgency that made the project exciting as well as worthwhile," Jim Prior said.

Then October 1st arrived. John Cardinal Dearden introduced Bishop Dempsey to the newsmen and women. The press conference was held in the archdiocesan offices at 211 East Chicago Avenue. Approximately thirty members of the press were in attendance. These included virtually all the major Chicago dailies, local and network television stations, a number of radio stations, AP, UPI, and the *New York Times*, among others.

The bishop was immediately barraged with questions about whether the campaign was offered as an alternative to government funding. "The campaign," Bishop Dempsey explained, "is not intended to replace or duplicate existing welfare or charities programs. One of the intended effects is to spur the government to faster action and progress in alleviating what should be the major concern of our time."

"The purpose of the drive," Cardinal Dearden added, "is to raise funds and to change hearts."

"Listening to the poor" was to be the key of the campaign. The primary thrust of the drive was to allow the poor to tell the Church what improvements were needed, and then to have the Church follow up with action.

Bishop Dempsey went on to tell the reporters that "The tradition of churches in helping the poor is a long and honorable one; so also is the tradition of the poor aiding themselves . . . but the poor have been vastly unheralded, frequently thwarted, often underestimated.

"None of society's current priorities are more important than the dignity and well-being of any individual human person," he added.

When a member of the press asked if the Church intended, in dealing with the poor, to impose the Catholic birth control teaching, he answered, "The Church isn't going to move into poverty areas and tell the people how many children to have. But, let us remember, that the poor often look at their children as their greatest riches.

"The self-help funds," he pointed out, "will be used to organize the poor economically and politically within their own communities. They will go to helping the poor to move and assimilate themselves into the mainstream of American society."

By mid-afternoon, the word was out about the campaign. My brother, who was already a busy man in the Chicago area, would now take on full-time responsibility on a national level. It has been said that faith is the elixir of youth. The bishop, at the age of fifty-two, his short curly hair now completely silver-gray, stepped into his new position with an all-consuming zeal.

CHAPTER FIFTEEN

A CRUSADE IS LAUNCHED

WITHIN A FEW days after the Campaign for Human Development was announced, Michael set out with his task force on a six-city tour of the nation. In each city they were to meet with a team representing all the dioceses in that particular region. Airport motels were used for the meetings, to facilitate scheduling.

The first of the meetings was held in Chicago, near O'Hare Airport. The campaign directors from Illinois, Indiana, Michigan, and Ohio attended. They were addressed by Cardinal Cody and Michele Cardinal Pellegrino, Archbishop of Turin, who was visiting the United States, as well as Bishop Dempsey. Bishop Dempsey brought some friends with him, including Robert Squires and Robert LeFlore.

A film was used to open the meeting, and spots were also played for information and background. As was planned for all sessions, a great effort was placed in involving the local Ordinaries in the campaign. Here and in many cities, the Ordinaries themselves came and spoke to the group.

Bishop Dempsey spoke on the overall dimensions of the campaign and touched on some of the substantive issues that were inherent in its development. Mr. Beusse addressed himself to the educational and promotional side of the campaign. Mr. Mc-Sweeney spoke on the role of the campaign director insofar as raising the funds from each diocese and parish was concerned. Mr. Cosgrove spoke on the social side of the question. He discussed dimensions of poverty in this country and gave specific indications of how the campaign could help in this fight, as well as giving some of the specifics about the management and methodology of the campaign. Mr. Prior spoke on the public information aspects.

The tour took them from Chicago to Denver, then to San Francisco, to Houston, to Atlanta, and finally to New York. Regional meetings were scheduled two or three days apart and the presentations were repeated in each city.

Each session was followed by a press conference. At the press conference there would be perhaps three television crews, several radio news teams, and religion editors from the local newspapers. Positive stories about the campaign would follow. After that, Michael would be off to participate in television and radio interviews. He made his first television talk-show appearance in Denver on the much-watched "High Noon" program. There was a concentrated effort to localize these appearances. In each one, Michael would focus on some of the local self-help programs for the poor that seemed to be achieving good results in the city where he was speaking.

In San Francisco, he had the first of his experiences on a call-in show. This was Bob Dornan's radio program on KGO. The host for this call-in show is now a Congressman from Los Angeles.

In San Francisco and in Houston, local Spanish-speaking groups came to present their views or to hear Bishop Dempsey explain the thrust of the campaign. Mutually helpful ideas were exchanged. As a result, Antonio Tinajero, director of the Spanish-speaking division of the United States Catholic Council's Department of Social Development, crystallized the need for more emphasis on telling the campaign story through the Spanish-speaking media, as well as developing Spanish-language promotional materials. Later, many proposals for self-help funding emanated from Spanish-speaking groups.

Representatives from fourteen states gathered for the meeting in Atlanta on October 14. There was the same kind of enthusiastic response to the presentations, and the media followed up with wide publicity.

On October 16, the campaign team held the final in the series of regional meetings at the Holiday Inn at La Guardia Airport in New York.

Terence Cardinal Cooke, Archbishop of New York, spoke to campaign directors from eight states. Even the campaign director from Guam attended because he was so motivated by the Associated Press wire story that resulted from the October 1st press conference. Bishop Francis Mugavero, of Brooklyn, and the Most Reverend Joseph F. Donnelly, Auxiliary Bishop of Hartford, also attended.

At the press conference, which was held just before the campaign meeting, ABC channel 7 "Eyewitness News" was present and did a segment that evening on television. Also present were representatives from the *New York Daily News*, UPI, Religious News Service, WOR Radio, and the *Catholic News*. The New York campaign directors' meeting proved to be the largest in the series, with over fifty campaign directors in attendance.

Then Michael returned to Chicago, where Father Roache

kept him busy with six television and radio commitments. We viewed Mike on television in his home surroundings as he drove through the streets of Lawndale, pointing out the needs of his own community. He saw Lawndale as a vast mine filled with precious jewels still waiting to be brought to the surface and polished. All they needed was opportunity. Even so-called "down-time" — the unscheduled time — was fast-paced and the momentum kept building toward the time for the campaign collection.

By October 23, the team was in headquarters in the nation's capital. A decision was made to hold another series of regional meetings. Round Two got underway in Washington, D.C., with a presentation for the professional staff of the USCC. St. Louis, Boston, Baltimore, and Los Angeles would follow.

Meanwhile, back in New York, all during these regional trips, other campaign task force workers were making arrangements for Bishop Dempsey with the local and national media in that city. Joan Paul, who had written speeches for the bishop, handled the production of campaign programs.

At various intervals, Michael flew to New York to appear on shows or to be interviewed. He appeared on a forty-five-minute conversation on Arlene Francis' show on WOR, which was broadcast over one hundred and thirty-nine stations.

Joan Paul also arranged for him to appear on NBC's "Analogue" program on November 4. Michael spoke out emphatically, saying, "The bishops have asked me to lead a nationwide campaign for Catholics that will build up to a crescendo by November 22, to bring to the attention of Catholic people all over America, first of all, the myths of poverty, because there are so very many. We fold our hands piously and say that the poor will always be with us. The testimony of history is that the poor go away and they develop. They get into a better way of life and they disappear, not because they are ignored, but because opportunity is opened for them. But that happens no longer. In our society the poor will be poor forever, not because of our piety, but because we refuse to open doors of opportunity to them. I just refuse to say that this is a sociological problem. To me, poverty in America is a religious and an ethical problem."

In the course of the discussion he answered a statement concerning our country's priorities. "It's a terrible thing to say, given the concern about damage to the environment, but to me smoking factories are a sign of jobs; and maybe we can have all those factories without the smoke. But I'd hate to get so involved in the smoke that we forget the human lives that are deprived of basic necessities just because we feel that we can solve the problems of ecology but can't solve the very human problems of poor people. So, I'm all for the other priorities the country has established in the last few years, but I think the Campaign for Human Development intensifies the fact that if we are going to go with pride to the solution of other problems in our civilization, we can't put the poor last on our priority list."

My brother returned to Chicago the following day. While still in the airport, he checked in with Cardinal Cody's office by phone.   Of course Mike knew that Richard Cardinal Cushing of Boston had died on Monday of that week. Now Mike was asked to represent Chicago at the funeral, since Cardinal Cody had a previous commitment. Although he had been looking forward to a few days' rest inbetween his travels, Mike called Lourdes and asked Father Purtell to bring him a change of clothes. Then he boarded a plane and was back in the air.

Indeed, during his absences, Michael depended on Father Pehler and Father Purtell to keep the parish running smoothly; and they attended to the needs of all.

Soon the energetic task force, including Bishop Dempsey, was on the road for the added round of cities. They proceeded to St. Louis, Boston, and then to Baltimore.

On the morning of November 11, Michael was in Baltimore. By mid-afternoon he was in Chicago. By midnight he was in Los Angeles. The reason for his trip back to Chicago was his commitment to speak at the thirtieth annual Lecture Bureau Dinner of the Archdiocesan Union of Holy Name Societies of Chicago. Naturally, his subject was the Campaign for Human Development.

The task force met him in Los Angeles, and the following day Mike appeared at a press conference. Then, using the telephone, he taped a report for the Spanish broadcasting network, which was beamed into Spanish-language stations throughout the nation.

During the weeks when the campaign crew traveled and worked together, a great mutual respect and admiration developed among them. Each observed the complete dedication of his fellow members to their common cause. They would begin each day at Mass, either in Bishop Dempsey's hotel room or in a nearby church. Some of the men who had been altar boys in their youth, were happy for the opportunity to serve Mass again; and especially the Mass of the bishop who was the spokesman for the poor.

The next big day for the Campaign for Human Development was November 16, the opening day of the National Council of Catholic Bishops' general meeting in Washington, D.C. In the opening session, Cardinal Dearden gave a moving and eloquent address on the urgent need for all Catholics to support the campaign. By so doing, the cardinal once again — as he had done in Chicago — articulated the high priority of the campaign throughout the Catholic Church of the United States. It was a tremendously impressive speech, and since the meeting was open to the press for the opening session, it was widely quoted. But all was not roses at this Bishops' Meeting, as far as the Campaign for Human Development was concerned.

On the previous day, the National Association of Laymen (NAL) had held a press conference to urge the Church and the bishops to make more open disclosures of the Church's "wealth." They indirectly linked the campaign to this request, charging that the Church was going to the collection baskets for the poor when it actually already had the resources to do something about poverty.

The story broke in the press, on local television, and — most damaging of all — on Walter Cronkite's evening broadcast on CBS. It was the first major negative report on the campaign. The impression was given that somehow laymen, or this association of laymen, were against the campaign collection. The timing could not have been worse — just a week before the November 22nd collection. The campaign staff task force went to work to set the record straight.

Ben Kubasik, who had worked earlier to gain television placements for Bishop Dempsey, collaborated with others in drafting a statement for Michael. It read in part, "The Catholic Bishops of the United States are heartsick at the thought that the allegations of fringe groups might jeopardize the Church's campaign, which involves a national collection in all the Catholic churches in the United States, next Sunday, November 22nd."

Then Charles Reilly, under whose direction the National Catholic Office of Radio and Television had handled contacts with the network radio and television stations for regular religious programming for the campaign, went to top officials of the Columbia Broadcasting System. He protested the cavalier and inaccurate reporting of this particular program and asked for a correction or at least a clarification of the facts.

Although Walter Cronkite did not carry Bishop Dempsey's rebuttal as originally taped for CBS-TV, he did — on the November 17 broadcast — put the issue in a light much more favorable to the campaign and to the Church, and he called attention to the imminent collection date in a positive manner. In terms of public relations, this resulted in a net gain from the viewpoint of campaign officials.

The irony of the situation was that a day or so later, the NAL issued a press release asking Catholics to contribute generously to the campaign, which it called "a much-needed effort and an appropriate use of Church resources."

Some other events at the Bishops' Meeting involved the campaign. Bishop Mugavero made the interim report of the ad hoc committee on Human Development and released the nominations for the forty-member National Committee on Human Development. Shortly thereafter, this was released to the press. The names and biographical sketches of committee members were made available. The release detailed the makeup of the committee, pointing out that twenty-four states were represented. Four members were bishops. Eleven were priests or religious. The remaining twenty-five were laymen. Eight were women. Twenty-six white persons, five blacks, one Indian, and eight Spanish-speaking persons were on the committee.

Bishop Dempsey made his report to the full body of bishops on Thursday, November 19. He paid special tribute to all who had labored so hard for the campaign, from the Ordinaries and campaign directors to the task force and to all involved in the campaign. He placed special emphasis on the help that poor people had already rendered in advising and endorsing this campaign. Finally, he acknowledged his great thanks to his key aides who had brought something very meaningful and impressive from ground zero in a few short weeks.

An estimated one thousand volunteers were officially working to see that the Campaign for Human Development achieved its goals, while many others worked in informal and unofficial capacities to assist it. Now was the time for the confluence of activity to insure that all elements moved down their different tracks the way they were supposed to. October 1 was over; the regional tour was over; the additional trips to five cities were over, the Bishops'

Meeting was over; and now all eyes were turned to November 22.

The day came; and the collection was taken. The bishops' crusade was a phenomenal success. People really cared about the poor. They cared enough to contribute eight and a half million dollars. In the history of the American Church, this was the largest sum ever amassed in a special collection.

Opening day for nationwide Campaign for Human Development (October 1, 1970). Bishop Michael R. Dempsey speaks to national press conference in Chicago. In the foreground are John Cardinal Dearden of Detroit, President of the National Conference of Catholic Bishops, and Robert B. Beusse, the conference's Director of Communication. These leaders inspired many others to join in the Campaign for Human Development that is an ever continuing effort.

CHAPTER SIXTEEN

INVESTING IN THE POOR

THE FIRST CAMPAIGN collection had been accomplished. Immediately the major task of allocating the funds began. Thirteen hundred proposals were submitted requesting campaign funds. Now my brother had to oversee the carrying out of the campaign's promises.

As soon as the receipts of the national collection were tabulated, the criteria for obtaining funds from the Campaign for Human Development were announced by the Washington office.

Most of those benefitting from a project had to be from low-income groups;

The poor had to have the dominant voice in any self-help project;

Funding would not be considered for projects which could be adequately funded by monies known to be already available from the private or public sector;

The project or activity for which funding was requested must conform to the moral teaching of the Church;

High priority for funding was given to promising, innovative projects which would demonstrate a change from traditional approaches to poverty.

High priority was also extended to projects which would directly benefit a large number of people rather than a few, and to projects which would foster cooperation among and within diverse groups.

Grants would be made annually and monies disbursed quarterly upon receipt of a satisfactory progress report. Proposals requesting at least ten thousand dollars, but not more than two hundred thousand dollars, would be considered.

Here in Chicago, the bishop appointed an advisory board consisting of people he knew personally, people who lived in the inner-city and who would have the necessary empathy to study the proposals judiciously. He hand-carried these requests for campaign funds to the committee when it met in the Catholic Charities building at Twelfth and Wabash. The committee remained in session on the first day from nine in the morning until midnight.

Robert LeFlore recalls, "We were aiming for programs that would benefit the greatest number of people. Some were programs wherein people in the depressed areas could receive training. I think we made a very good selection."

Among those selected was an agency called Just Jobs, with offices on North Broadway, in Mike's former neighborhood. This agency was made viable by the funds appropriated through the campaign.

The Just Jobs office was opened with the hope of breaking the cycle of despair commonly associated with day-labor operations. John Plunkett, an Uptown resident who was the very competent manager of Just Jobs, received the initial funding of a twenty-four thousand, seven hundred-dollar loan from the Campaign for Human Development. This was a high-risk undertaking, but the loan gave it credibility so that it could get other grants in the future.

Another of the successful projects funded in the Chicago area was OJT — Opportunities Through Jobs in Trucking. This was an ideal example of a self-help project. The program, which received a fifty thousand-dollar grant from the campaign, initially trained men from minority groups to be dock workers. Soon this project expanded into a tractor-trailer drivers' program.

But before it got underway, Bishop Dempsey was forming an association that would function as the funding agent for the trucking program.

He invited about twelve men, all of whom were active community people on the Westside, to attend a Sunday afternoon meeting. After greeting the men, he explained that he had called them together to present still another aspect of the campaign for their consideration. He went on to say that he wished to form a Catholic Laymen's Association in order to place the responsibility of the distribution of funds for a particular program into capable hands. He asked for their help. Bill Kirkpatrick was among those attending. "Then he came up with the trucking thing," Bill recalls.

The men who were assembled were very willing to work with the bishop, and in April of 1971, the Catholic Laymen's Association was incorporated. About twenty black parishes were soon represented in the association.

Mike had been checking out places which he possibly could rent for a truck drivers' training site. Then Charles Bidwell, the owner of Sportsman's Park Race Track, came along and generously donated the use of his race track's parking lot for a training center. The campaign's seed money was used to buy the trucks.

Monroe Sullivan had left the Tri-Faith office and was now the owner and director of Trainco, Inc. — Manpower Training for Industry, which was both a school and a placement agency in a downtown location. His company contracted to train the prospective truck drivers. After Trainco instructed the people and got them licensed, the Catholic Laymen took care of the finances.

It was an intensive five-week course, after which the men were ready to be placed in jobs paying between two hundred and fifty and three hundred dollars a week. This instantly took them out of the poverty level.

Moreover, each man who completed the course pledged that after he found employment, he would pay the five hundred-dollar tuition fee for another trainee. Each week there were more checks coming in from the men who were already on the road. They were proud to help someone else.

"The thing turned out to be terrific," Bill remembers. Within a relatively short amount of time, one hundred minority men found that the way out of poverty was by truck.

The bishop's responsibilities also involved hearing the problems that inevitably arise when the funds available are not sufficient to satisfy all the requests. After the campaign money had been allotted, Michael received a complaint from a Catholic group in southern California which was dissatisfied with the funding.

Bishop Dempsey was informed that a representative would be coming to Chicago to voice the grievances of this particular organization. The representative flew into O'Hare, and after checking into a downtown hotel, phoned the bishop to ask for an appointment. He suggested that they meet in a private dining room of a restaurant.

Mike said, "Why don't you come out here to my rectory for lunch? My office is here for any information we might need."

"All right. I'll be there at eleven-thirty," the man answered.

A while later, Michael received another call. It was his luncheon guest, calling to say that when he gave the Lourdes' address to a cab driver, the cabbie said, "I'm afraid to go into that neighborhood." Mike's guest had decided that he didn't want to go into that neighborhood either; but Mike convinced him to try another driver. Soon the fellow — a big strapping man — was getting out of a cab at 1444 South Keeler, and he had to walk around all the children who were playing in front of the rectory. He came in, much of the wind already out of his sails, and couldn't conceal his surprise at the National Director's place of residence. Mike assured him, "Oh, I have been pastor here for years."

Father Pehler and Father Purtell were waiting in the dining room, and the scene possessed its usual informality as Dorothy served them lunch. Apparently the visitor had anticipated pounding on the desk of a bishop who lived in elegant surroundings and telling him how the campaign money should be used. Now, while he lunched with the priests, he was obviously groping for words.

As they walked out of the dining room, Mike suggested, "Why don't you stop back again tomorrow?"

"Oh! No, no," the tall visitor responded. Then Mike graciously drove him back to the downtown hotel. I think the delegate returned to California with a better attitude toward the fund distribution.

In June of 1971, Father Robert V. Monticello was appointed to the newly-created post of executive director of the Campaign for Human Development. He was to head a Washington, D.C. staff of seven. Father Monticello had been the diocesan director of the campaign in Detroit and had a marvelous background in social development work. He and the bishop would work very closely together.

In the first year of the campaign, Monsignor Robert Hagarty had worked hard and well as our local director. But by the following year, he was pastor of a parish and also held a chancery job. Consequently, Michael took over, and, in effect, became the Chicago director as well as the national director.

At the time of the 1971 collection, Michael spoke about the success of the program.

"In the past year, while serving as national director of the campaign, I've been privileged to travel more than fifty thousand miles throughout the country, talking to poor people, listening to them, hearing and seeing both their problems and their aspirations. And from all this, the question inevitably arises: 'Has the campaign fulfilled the promises it has made to the poor of America? And where are we a year later?'

"I think we can best answer those questions by taking a look at some of the distinguishing marks of the Campaign for Human Development in its first year of performance:

"First, and I believe most important, the campaign has been educational in its approach. We have made use of every channel of communication: from the first-grade classroom to the mass electronic medium of network television and radio . . . and everything in between . . . to carry the one message: 'For God's sake, look at the poor, think about them, feel with them, work and share with them.'

"More than any other single thing, I believe the success or failure of this campaign will be measured in terms of how well it accomplishes its educational mission. The funding aspects are perhaps more visible, more tangible, but they must never be allowed to obscure or overshadow the primary goal of informing and educating.

"Secondly, I believe the campaign has established its credibility. In hundreds of communities throughout the country, from Maine to California, community leaders have let us know what their peoples' needs are. In every instance they have told us how campaign funds can best serve the interests of the poor in their communities.

"The Catholics of America have placed their trust in the campaign. They have given generously of their money, to be channeled through the Campaign Headquarters and the members of the National Committee, to the poor of America. The National Committee itself is composed largely of leaders from the poor communities, black, white, Spanish-speaking, representing all regional and ethnic backgrounds. The results of last November's collection are already at work in more than one hundred and fifty communities around the nation. Thousands of poor people are already experiencing the first fruits of the campaign's promise to support and finance self-help projects whose need the people themselves determined.

"Given the enormity of the need, whatever we have been able to do thus far, is only a small beginning, and we all have a long way to do, but we have begun and there is no turning back.

"The campaign has been, I think, a catalyst in the best sense of that word, by making it possible, through the use of campaign funds, for many community development projects to meet the eligibility requirements for additional state or federal funds. One of the more dramatic examples is the Military Highway Water Project in Texas. The campaign grant of one hundred and eighty thousand dollars enabled this most vital project to qualify for an additional long-term government loan of almost four million dollars."

He added that he hoped that the campaign had begun to act

as a catalytic agent, by encouraging individuals, groups, and movements, to build a new, ever-broadening basis for understanding, and by helping the poor to develop a stronger sense of self-determination and eventually, self-sufficiency.

Seven million, four hundred and eighty-two thousand, seven hundred dollars was raised in the 1971 collection. Jim Prior said later, "If a Most Valuable Player had been picked for the campaign team, the title would have gone to our leader, Bishop Dempsey. He translated the campaign from a gleam in some bishops' eyes to the reality it became."

CHAPTER SEVENTEEN

DEMPSEY, THE DIPLOMAT

A PRIEST WHO worked with the Campaign for Human Development once called Mike a radical. He added, "If ever a priest had the right formula to make the inner-city Church stay alive, it was Mike Dempsey. He had what it took to mold things together." Surely Mike made the kinds of innovative changes that no one else would; and in so doing, gave people a chance to make it on their own and not be dependent.

He constantly communicated a tremendous spirit of hope. At one time, he commented, "Perhaps I am one of the few optimists around, but my optimism is based on people, not on programs." And, indeed, his optimism made people true believers.

Looking back now, I feel that I had, and perhaps all the family had, a great lack of sensitivity as far as Mike's life was concerned. We didn't suspect that there were many heartaches connected with his work; and we never would have known if people had not come forward in later years to tell us. Nothing was easy for him. We always knew about the activities in which he was involved and how important they were to him. We knew too that his average work day was so strenuous that if ever we wanted to contact him, it would have to be before eight in the morning, because after that hour it would be hard to locate him. Through the years he was ever available to listen to our problems; but in his love for us at home, he told us only the pleasant part of his life.

One incident — which we learned of only after his death — must have been very painful to him. Immediately following the announcement that he was to become a bishop, a group of priests visited him and asked him to decline the appointment. I don't know their reason. Possibly they couldn't envision him doing the work they felt had to be done. At that time Michael very calmly assured them that he had no inclination to decline, and that he expected to use the office of bishop to accomplish much for God's poor.

But, by his own choice, Michael never shared his personal hurts with us; nor did he tell us of the problems and the dangers which were part of his life. If we had known that some people were unkind to him, we would have expressed deep concern and understanding. It would seem that for him to keep hurt feelings

124

and aggravations within himself must have been an added suffering. But that was Mike — he wouldn't want us to know anything that might make us unhappy; and he surely wouldn't want us to worry about his safety.

Michael was a prayerful man; and the priests who lived with him observed that no matter how busy he was, he always allotted much time for prayer. Considering this, I am sure that the consolation he received directly from God was sufficient; so that he really didn't need our sympathy. Whenever he came home to us, our Father D was happy and relaxed, although sometimes so tired that he would fall asleep in a chair.

The part of Mike's life that we never knew, has since evolved through the recollections of people who knew him in a way that we never could. During the publicity phase of the Campaign for Human Development, his name was emphasized as "Dempsey, the fighter for the poor." And, because of the responsibilities he accepted in that cause, Mike had to be a scrapper. But though he had power, he used it in a very diplomatic way. He regarded every man and woman he ever met as one of God's children, and he never forgot this — not even in heated debates, nor in political maneuvering.

He consistently used the office of bishop in a very positive way to help the poor. This is what he considered to be the true spirit of the Church; and he worked with an all-consuming fervor. Some priests loved him for it; some saw it as a challenge to be aspired to; and others regarded him with some animosity. Certain people couldn't accept the fact that a person in his position could be so totally selfless.

Because of his deep involvement in the archdiocesan inner-city work, the Chicago Conference on Religion and Race, the Campaign for Human Development, and various other programs, it was Bishop Dempsey's duty to appoint or hire people and to observe their progress. Scores of religious and lay men and women reported directly to him.

Mike operated in such a way that people made decisions for themselves. This is something that very many clergy, very many executives, and even the top leaders in our country, cannot say — that they have enough confidence in their people that they will let them make decisions — and make decisions that are right.

He had a natural "feel" for people. Mike concentrated on raising leaders from among those involved in a program, so that as soon as the program developed, he himself would no longer be needed. And there was always another program beginning.

If Mike found that a person was not able to make a decision, or not able to keep his word, Mike would replace him or have him replaced; but this was always accomplished in a very kind way. The person would normally resign. He would not be fired. This would assure the individual of keeping his pride. The bishop would confront the person with a situation in such a way that the man would say, "I can't handle it." But he would never be fired.

Even as I prepared to write my brother's biography, many of the people I interviewed, told me: "It was Dempsey who got me going in my career."

These were days of great agitation within the black community. Mike, as the Church's inner-city bishop, took upon himself the responsibility of mediating disputes. On one occasion, an angry group was attempting to take over an inner-city parish. Cardinal Cody was about ready to close down the church. But Bishop Dempsey wasn't going to let this happen. This church belonged to the people; not to any one group. Mike decided that when these black militants called their next meeting, he would attend and try to speak to the assembly. The word got around.

Early on the evening when the meeting was to be held, a station wagon drove up in front of Mike's rectory. Five men of the immediate area had come to escort the bishop. The bishop sat in the middle of the front seat, surrounded by his volunteer escorts, who were ready to intercede if necessary, and prevent any violence.

It was expected that about three hundred people would attend this meeting. As the men entered the hall, someone commented about the bishop's bringing his bodyguards. Mike said, "You fellows stay back here in the vestibule." Though the atmosphere was frightening, he walked right in.

The men accompanying him did as he requested. But from the vestibule they sent for the ringleaders, and a spokesman from the escorts warned: "If you do anything to degrade the bishop we will break up the meeting."

Bishop Dempsey was able to listen to the people and to speak to them. There was not complete agreement, but the fact that he was able to communicate for the Church was some accomplishment.

In the early 1970s, a new kind of inner-city Church movement began. In an attempt to stabilize their neighborhoods, parishes were uniting in what were called "parish clusters." Anywhere from five to ten parishes with similar interests and similar problems would unite for the purpose of moral support in solving their difficulties. The parishes that worked together were not necessarily close geographically. Many parishes were represented in the clusters only by their priests, but some included Sisters and lay people.

There were times when the cluster meetings developed into heated or angry sessions. Bishop Dempsey was the trouble-shooter for the archdiocese. He went to straighten out trouble anywhere.

Though the bishop always encouraged people to get together and work out their problems, he was sometimes unwelcome at the cluster meetings. A meeting could become a springboard from which those who were attempting to reorganize the Westside, would thrust all their frustrations and all their anger at him because he was an authority figure. He represented the Church and the cardinal as well as the inner-city and the black population.

Mike had a mind that instantly grasped situations. As the archdiocesan representative he never wanted to be any kind of a "boss." In fact, many people say that it was his low profile that made him successful. He respected the opinions of others and involved them in decision-making. He could understand their hostilities and he tried to channel them into positive action through arbitration. He didn't lose his calm and he didn't lose his perspective. As one priest said, "Mike attempted to solve everything with 'sweet reasonableness.'" At the same time, my brother always defended the authority of the cardinal in archdiocesan matters.

He consistently averted confrontation. Mike could listen silently to insults from those who were fighting the whole social system, and emerge with no ill-feeling. He knew that a person who couldn't put his finger on the source of a problem might have a need to blame someone. And if anyone had to let off steam, it didn't bother Mike in the slightest to be the target.

Because he lived in the inner-city, Mike had a ringside seat as the Church's representative. Cardinal Cody had many consultants in residence at Holy Name Cathedral. These were priests who were involved in various archdiocesan agencies. But if the cardinal had a problem involving a basic decision, he would eventually confer with Bishop Dempsey.

There were times when priests who were responsible for

Church finances, worked with Mike. One such instance occurred when two long-established schools, Providence High School for Girls and St. Mel's High School for Boys, were both in financial trouble. White students no longer attended these schools, and the black enrollment was not sufficient to support the schools. It seemed that the practical solution was to close both buildings.

But Michael would never consent to this. He felt that the Westside must have local Catholic high schools. Soon he was developing an idea for merging the two schools. With the approval of the archdiocese and the school authorities, a new Providence-St. Mel coeducational high school was instituted in the Providence building. To this day it has a fine scholastic rating.

And, during these early 1970s, there were also problems at another level of the Catholic educational system. The grade schools were operating under great stress. The inner-city schools scored deficits ranging from seven thousand dollars to as high as ninety-eight thousand dollars. It was indeed a catastrophic problem to the archdiocese.

Mike was soon to be instrumental in initiating the concept "Operation Friendship." This developed from meetings with Bishop McManus and the school board. Mike was asked to co-ordinate the program. There was to be an ongoing commitment, whereby a parish that was financially solvent would adopt a struggling parish and send subsidies directly to that parish. It was called the "twinning" of parishes, and it had the potential for being a far-reaching apostolate.

Each pastor was free to work out with his parish board the method of contribution, provided that his parishioners were able and willing to participate. In some cases, racial prejudice was a factor in a parish's refusal.

At an organizational meeting, Mike stressed the point that, on an average, black parents paid more in tuition for the education of their youngsters than did white parents.

He said, "The problem which predominantly black parishes face is their inability to generate any substantial parish subsidy for the school because the parish is so small. In white parishes, only about one-third to one-half of the parishioners have children in school. In predominantly black parishes, however, the vast majority of parishioners have children in school, leaving very few other people to help support the school.

"Family for family, inner-city people are giving far more to

the Church and to their schools than any comparable group anywhere. Their sacrifices, their generosity in sustaining their schools
and in sending their young people through high school, is one of
the greatest stories of sacrifice and deep love for the Church that
you will ever find."

As coordinator, it was Mike's duty to contact the parishes
that were being asked to share, and convince them to participate.
It was also his job to arrange which parish was to twin with which
other parish. Every time he spoke for this cause, he reminded his
listeners that the clergy and the people of the smaller parishes
were doing their best, and they well deserved the admiration of
those who wished to help them. He insisted that it be a parish-to-
parish commitment and that no one in-between "count the chips."

Pairing of parishes had a potential for many personal relation-
ships between priests and people in acts of genuine Christian
charity which went beyond financial help.

It was hoped that the principal beneficiaries would be the
donors, who would be spiritually motivated to help others in the
name of their Lord. For many people, this was an opportunity to
rise to a challenge far beyond what would have been expected
of them.

Bishop McManus was the pastor of St. Ferdinand's Church on
the Northwest side of Chicago. He and my brother planned the
twinning of St. Ferdinand's and Our Lady of Lourdes.

Before Bishop McManus proposed the twinning program to
his parishioners, he set aside a full afternoon to talk with Bishop
Dempsey about what would be the most urgent needs of Our Lady
of Lourdes. Expecting Michael to tell him that he needed money
for salaries, utilities and other constant expenses, Bishop McManus
was surprised and delighted when Michael said that he had high
hopes that some financial assistance from St. Ferdinand's would
enable him to paint and decorate the interior of Lourdes' Church.
Michael also asked for some help to refurbish the school's lunch
room, which had a dingy appearance.

Before Lent in 1970, Bishop McManus told the St. Ferdin-
and's parishoners about the needs of Our Lady of Lourdes and
invited them to divide their Sunday contributions, half and half,
between the two parishes. Each parishioner was asked to make a
personal decision about this request and to indicate a desire for
this division by placing a card in the regular Sunday envelopes for
the six Sundays of Lent.

"The response was amazing," Bishop McManus said. "During that Lent and every Lent thereafter, St. Ferdinand's parishioners contributed approximately fifteen thousand dollars to Our Lady of Lourdes.

"I vividly recall Bishop Dempsey's visit to the parish to thank the people for their gift. Many of the parishioners presumed that the bishop would give a long 'begging talk' and would lecture the congregation about their obligation to help black people. All the bishop said was: 'The parishioners of Our Lady of Lourdes had a gloriously happy Easter when they celebrated the Eucharist in their beautiful church, newly-painted blue to honor Our Lady of Lourdes. They thank you for your help for this and other good things at Lourdes. I thank you too.' Then the bishop gave a superb homily on the Gospel of the day. After the Masses, the parishioners crowded around him to thank him for his sermon and to tell him that they wanted to continue their help for Lourdes."

This twinning program was part of the beautiful narrative of the generosity of the people of God. "For various reasons there has never been a list published of all the twinning or Operation Friendship parishes," Bishop Dempsey said in the summer of 1972. "I believe that charity isn't shouted from the housetop. Parishes are welcome to talk about their charity if they like, but it is a relationship whereby the parish that offers, looks for no recognition, no name in any official communique. It offers charity the way it should be offered — so the receiver knows but nobody else. The better part of three hundred thousand dollars a year exchanges hands between parishes; and it hasn't slowed down. About sixty parishes are now involved in Operation Friendship."

Wonderful successes came out of the inner-city apostolate. Among them was the priestly work of Father George Clements, whom Cardinal Cody assigned to Holy Angels' parish, at 607 Oakwood Boulevard. Father Clements possessed youthful enthusiasm and a great amount of ability to work well with people.

The education of the young was the priest's special concern. In future years, his parish produced a remarkable number of seminarians. Father Clements received national recognition when the *Wall Street Journal* wrote about the school's outstanding academic rating. The newspaper credited the pastor with using old-fashioned teaching methods to achieve this status.

As soon as Father Clements could see the fruits of his efforts in the parish, he invited Bishop Dempsey to visit and to share in

his joy. He said that he regarded the bishop as a real light and bea-
con of hope to so many people. "He was always identified with
the poor. No matter how many honors were bestowed upon him,
Bishop Dempsey was still the Bishop of the Poor. This is to his
everlasting credit."

In an interview, Michael once said: "In the inner-city of Chicago you have a great group of dynamic priests, religious and laymen, who are totally committed to the better life of people who
are living in poverty, and yet have the same hopes and aspirations
for self-determination that people consider necessary for a truly
human life.

"I would say," he continued, "that the poor people in our
many inner-city parishes have the dynamism and energy to attack
the root causes of our problems, and have come up with some of
the finest solutions to problems that you can find anywhere in the
United States.

"We have not settled merely for child care or tutoring. We do
know that education is a great part of the first step toward freedom and a better life — but poor people have also tackled the
problems of better jobs, better housing, and greater determination
in the political activity of their own communities. And, in all of
this, the Church is working with them. The Catholic Church has
done something to change the picture in the desperate communities."

CHAPTER EIGHTEEN

"HE WAS THERE WHEN HE WAS NEEDED"

GENE CALLAHAN ONCE said, "Anyone can give you a hundred vignettes about what Mike did, but in summing him up, I remember reading an article that was written on the day of Winston Churchill's funeral. As the boat was carrying Churchill's body down the Thames, a writer named Jimmy Breslin was sitting in a pub, talking the barman, while all the high and mighty people were at the funeral. He asked the inn-keeper, 'What did you think of Churchill?'

"The fellow looked at him and said, 'Well, he was there when he was needed.'

"That's what Mike was. Whenever things were going on, if you looked around, he was there if he was needed. He never received publicity, nor sought it; he just knew what was to be done and he did it."

Mike was needed again when Baird and Warner had located a site at Thirty-Fifth Street and the lakefront for another low-income housing project. The realtors had purchased part of the site from the Department of Urban Renewal, and other parts from private owners. However, this amount of land was still not adequate for the buildings they had planned.

The remaining section of the site belonged to Catholic Charities, and their representatives had clearly stated that they did not wish to sell.

Catholic Charities operated a home for retarded children on this location. The adjacent land, which the Sisters of St. Joseph owned, had been purchased for another purpose, but it had not worked out as expected. It was this space that the builders needed.

Bishop Dempsey offered to visit the Sisters and discuss the issue with them. Consequently, he was instrumental in helping them decide that if they were not going to use the land as they originally planned, then selling it to the realtors would be the best thing for them to do.

He also had to convince them that family housing units in their immediate vicinity would not have an adverse affect upon the children.

As a result, John Baird, Elzie Higginbottom, and the Baird and Warner Realtors, were able to arrange the purchase of the land. Then the builders proceeded to erect the beautiful Lake Park Manor apartments adjoining Douglas Park.

Michael had become chairman of the Conference on Religion and Race, and he worked wholeheartedly for its causes. His friend, Father Ray Cusak, from neighboring Presentation parish, was on the Conference too. He had succeeded Monsignor Jack Egan, who left Presentation in the spring of 1970 to take on a special assignment at the University of Notre Dame.

Father Cusak remembers the all-day sessions that would drag on until finally he would be dropping the bishop off at Lourdes at nine-thirty at night. They would be exhausted.

Then Mike would get into his own car to make some house-calls before returning to his rectory. He always had people in mind whom he had to visit.

On the following morning Mike would arrive at the Conference with the synopsis of the previous day's meeting and the plan for this day's agenda. He had typed it himself. His energy was boundless.

In the Conference meetings, Michael always wanted to eliminate lengthy discussion and any kind of red tape. If something seemed to be for the good of the poor, he would say, "Just do it."

Many eminent people served on the Conference board. All were devoted to helping their fellow-man. The Right Reverend James W. Montgomery, the Episcopal Bishop of Chicago, was a very active member of the board. He recalls, "Mike could be impassioned on some point and thoroughly profound, and yet always had a wonderful way of bringing a twinkle to his eye and saying something that would relieve the tension and make people laugh. He always seemed to be a man who combined sanctity, true piety, deep pastoral concern for individuals, with the broadest social conscience that I have ever seen. It was a wonderful combination, and he exemplified all of it throughout his priestly and episcopal life.

"Certainly he lived the spirit of the post-Vatican II Roman Catholic Church as far as his dealings with his "separated brethren" were concerned. There was no narrowness of spirit but only an all-embracing love and desire to work together in God's name."

Robert Lamson was another member who can reminisce about Mike's days at the helm. Mr. Lamson was a representative of the Presbytery of Chicago to the Conference board. His field of activity was in executive search and placement of people. He had served on the Conference before the inception of Tri-Faith.

"Mike was just invaluable," Mr. Lamson remembers. "We couldn't have gotten it done without him. He was always available and interested; his judgments were good; and his evaluation of people was good. You just couldn't put a value on his contribution."

The work of the Conference branched out into many areas, always reaching to the needs of Chicago's underprivileged.

Another of its very worthwhile efforts involved the Cabrini Hospital at 811 South Lytle, near Circle Campus. Realizing that there was a need for a health center for low-income families residing in that area, and that no such facility existed, the Conference members were working on a plan to establish a clinic. They considered the Cabrini Hospital building the ideal location. Their next move was to convince the hospital staff to agree to an inner-city health center within the hospital.

Everyone on the Conference recognized Mike as a natural salesman wherever a program for the poor was concerned. And Mike was ever willing to let himself be used for a good cause. Consequently, he was the representative chosen to approach the hospital authorities with the proposal. The Sisters were greatly impressed by Bishop Dempsey's concern for the health care of the people who could be served. They agreed to the plan. And Sister Irma, who was the executive director of the Cabrini-Columbus-Cuneo Hospital group, and an outstanding woman in her field, and my brother became good friends.

However, the funding of the clinic did not develop as the Conference staff had expected. Michael was among those who flew to Washington to petition for a grant. They contacted Illinois senators Charles Percy and Adlai Stevenson; and Congressman Frank Annunzio and Roman Pucinski. They also spoke to the authorities at the Department of Health, Education, and Welfare. They were promised that the program was one of great priority and that it would move ahead aggressively. But, apparently, someone "torpedoed" it in a political move. Cabrini Clinic was never adequately funded by Washington. It was opened under the auspices of the Archdiocese of Chicago, rather than the Conference on Religion and Race.

It was said that, in his unusually quite but articulate way, Mike fired everyone to action, and kept the Conference afloat long after it might have sunk. In the latter days of his life, the Protestant denominations had run out of money, and there was a big split in the Church Federation. The problems of the State of Israel were an understandable distraction for the Jewish delegates. There was much discord among the black delegates because they felt they weren't represented in the Church Federation, which was dominated by the mainstream of Protestant denominations.

The Conference was in a perpetual budget crisis. The late Lee Gary, an attorney, was an anonymous benefactor. He was the chairman of the Archdiocesan Commission on Human Relations and Ecumenism. Father Edward Egan, who is now a monsignor assigned to the Chicago House in Rome, was the secretary of this commission, of which Mike was also a member. Father Egan describes Mr. Gary as "a splendid Catholic gentleman who was interested in the poor and the mistreated, and did everything he could to help them — for the love of Jesus Christ." Monsignor Egan worked with my brother on the Conference, the Ecumenism Commission, the Campaign for Human Development, and about twenty other committees.

"From 1968 to 1972," Monsignor Egan recalls, "I either saw or spoke on the telephone with Bishop Dempsey every day except Sunday, and sometimes also on Sunday. I never recall a single disagreement between us. Nor do I ever remember a single uncharitable word from him about anyone. He never permitted himself to become cynical or sarcastic."

Mayor Richard Daley long recognized Michael's dedication to the poor, and he assigned Mike to various citizens' committees. At the time of the first campaign collection, the mayor wrote: "I am asking you to serve on a Citizens' Committee (the Chicago Committee on Urban Opportunity) as a representative from the Archdiocese of Chicago. In this capacity you will be representing an agency which has long worked for the development of Chicago and its people. I am hopeful that you will be able to accept this appointment, as it is only with the participation and involvement of citizens like yourself that we can achieve the objectives of the Economic Opportunity Act, giving every individual an opportunity to work and live in decency and dignity."

Michael accepted the mayor's appointment and became a member of the citizens' committee. The Chicago Committee on Urban Opportunity was part of "The War on Poverty." This was in the heyday of that type of legislation — which is long gone.

Deton Brooks for years had been the director of research for the Cook County Department of Public Aid. When the War on Poverty began, the mayor had appointed Mr. Brooks director of the local Chicago Committee on Urban Opportunity.

Mr. Brooks might have preferred a kind of letterhead board. He likely didn't count on the gentle, soft-spoken bishop being one who would prod him unrelentingly for positive actions to benefit the poor.

Poverty programs routinely expended money for research and for surveys regarding the condition of the poor. Then more time would be given to deliberation before the people were actually helped. Mike was adamant in maintaining that every cent of the funds for the poor should be given directly to the poor and not to a sociologist who would analyze them. Indeed, he regarded some poverty programs as band-aid services — if people are hungry, give them food. Michael stressed helping people help themselves. The Lord, Himself, had given the example when He told the apostles, "Cast your line into the water."

Mike would say, "You teach people to fish instead of giving them fish."

On the Westside of Chicago, the proposed crosstown expressway was a boiling issue. Mayor Daley and big business were pro-crosstown, while thousands of homeowners living across the city in the shadows of Cicero Avenue were very much opposed to it. Churches of various denominations opened their halls for anti-crosstown meetings.

The cardinal could not publicly take a stand on the issue because it was a political one. But in 1972, all the Catholic pastors whose parishes lay within the proposed route, were summoned to a meeting downtown.

Charles Roche was a layman who accompanied his pastor to this meeting. Mr. Roche was one of the very dedicated leaders of the Citizens' Action Program. CAP, as it was called, had fought City Hall vehemently against the building of an expressway.

After listening to the discussion and getting the impression that the priests who were present were very unconcerned about whether or not crosstown would be built, Mr. Roche could no longer hold his peace. He rose, and stormed about the apathy of the priests, whose people would be losing their homes to crosstown. In retort, someone heatedly "told him off" and Mr. Roche felt utterly defeated. This was the one group from which he surely expected support for CAP.

Then, as the meeting ended, Bishop Dempsey came from behind and tapped Charles Roche on the shoulder, saying, "Will you wait for me? I'd like to go for a cup of coffee with you." This was the first time they met.

As they sipped their coffee, Bishop Dempsey said, "Charlie, you're a good man; but you'll have to learn to control your temper. You can accomplish everything if you just never let yourself get excited." Charlie didn't forget that advice, and he continued very successfully with the activities of CAP. To this day, crosstown has not been started.

CHAPTER NINETEEN

IN SIGHT OF THE FINISH LINE

IN THE SPRING of 1972 some changes took place in Our Lady of Lourdes' household. Father Pehler was transferred to a Southside parish and was succeeded by Father Raymond Jasinski. The first time our family met Father Jasinski was when we attended the annual "Thank You, Father Dempsey Dinner" which the Ladies' Auxiliary of the Knights of St. Peter Claver hosted at the Driftwood Restaurant. This celebration always took place on Fathers' Day, and it was most enjoyable for all.

Father Ray quickly fit into the parish scene; and he became a very close friend to my brother.

In July of that year, our family was saddened by the death of one of our members. Bill Hastings was on his way to work on a Saturday morning when he was killed in an automobile accident. It happened on the open road, Route 60, which he travelled daily. Bill was a maintenance man at St. Mary's parish in Lake Forest. He took pride in keeping the parish property in beautiful condition.

His younger boys, Mike and Jim, were at home when two police officers came with the sad tidings. The boys went along with the officers to notify Kay, who was working at McHenry Hospital's Medical Center.

It was a heartbreaking experience, not only for Kay and her family but for all of us. Bill was a most generous and kind man, and we all loved him.

Father Jasinski told us later that when Michael heard of Bill's death he completely broke down in grief, and he wept as though his heart was broken. Then he composed himself, cancelled all his appointments, and immediately drove out to Ingleside.

Michael remained with the Hastings for a week, during which time he was a great comfort to Kay, as well as being a help in making the arrangements and decisions which a sudden death entailed.

But soon he was back to his busy life again. He considered the Hastings his special responsibility and wanted to give the boys any spare time he could find, knowing that the loss of their father's companionship left a real void in their lives.

In September, Michael was invited to New York to receive the Good Samaritan Award for the year 1972. The National

Catholic Development Conference annually awarded to someone who epitomized the Christian endeavor to "liberate the human race from any oppressive situation" a beautiful statue of the Good Samaritan helping his needy brother. The award always went to a person whose life work embodied the spirit of the original Good Samaritan of the Gospel.

The bishop made the trip to the Americana Hotel and back the same day. At the Award luncheon, he said: "Thank you very much for this award you are giving me today, and for the great compliment it implies. Any person who seeks to serve others hopes to follow in the footsteps of the Good Samaritan."

He went on to say that the achievements of the Campaign for Human Development could never be attributed to any one person. "They can only result from teamwork. It has taken the efforts of all of us; the staff at our headquarters in Washington; the National Committee on Human Development, whose forty members are largely leaders from the poor communities across the country; the United States Bishops' Committee on Human Development; the Diocesan Campaign Directors; and all of our bishops and priests and Catholic people. We have worked together to give the Campaign for Human Development the success it has so far attained. The campaign has been a success because it has caught the spirit of this new expression of Love which is self-help — helping the poor to help themselves. It is the sign of the extraordinary generosity of American Catholics, who *do* take the poor seriously."

He added, "We have tried to help men understand that to love truly as Christians, we must give; for that is how we share in the Love and the Life of the Savior."

As fall approached, Michael was on the fund-raising trail for the Campaign for Human Development once more. The fruits of the first two collections were evident throughout the country. Among the numerous programs progressing as a result of campaign grants were: a crafts co-op started by rural whites in Bucksport County, Maine, after the area's only industry, a small shoe factory, failed; the job-training counselor funded at a vocational program for Chicano probationers, mostly drug offenders, in El Paso, Texas; a mobile meals service, featuring their native dishes, for elderly Chinese in San Francisco; and a food co-op run by Navajo Indians at a Pinon, Arizona reservation.

Just as in previous years, the campaign tour proceeded at a demanding pace. My brother, as a beggar for the poor, moved about the country in a whirlwind campaign, never allowing himself any time for sightseeing.

"The bishop had an incredible way of operating out of a telephone booth or a briefcase," Monroe Sullivan said. "He was just all over everywhere." Mike would laugh every time Moe commented, "You know, Bishop, for a bishop you're a hell of a guy."

Then, when Michael would return to the rectory between trips, Dorothy would say, "Bishop, you make it so interesting with all your coming and going."

Mike would answer, "Dorothy, I'd much rather be home."

She'd shake her head thoughtfully. "Bishop, there're no more like you," she would add.

And Mike would just smile.

Later Dorothy told me, "He was more tired than we knew."

Michael missed the people. His vocation to the priesthood was his most treasured gift from God. Being father of Lourdes' parish was his greatest pride.

At an evening Mass I heard him preach a sermon which I shall never forget. He was speaking to a small group of his parishioners, and his voice was strong and warm. He was apologetic about being away so much of the time. He explained that while his duties were taking him out of the city very often, he longed to be at home in Lawndale.

"You are my family and when I come back to you, many times I am very tired, just as any father coming home from his work is tired," he said. "I come to you for understanding and encouragement."

At the same time he missed his visits with us, his sisters and our families. He no longer took a day off as he had done in past years. But occasionally, when he found that he had about two hours to spare, he would call and say, "Ann, would you like to have an extra one for dinner?"

He would arrive, obviously fatigued, and sometimes I could detect asthma in his breathing. He usually sat at the kitchen table keeping me company while I prepared the food. The menu, even though it was "pot luck," always pleased him. There was nothing fancy about Bishop Mike.

Father Ray, too, noticed how often Michael suffered from asthma; but Michael never mentioned it.

Then, Sunday, November 12, arrived. It was the day for the third annual nationwide collection for the Campaign for Human

Development. We were glad that this particular task was completed once again, because we knew that it had been a very taxing few months for Father D.

Early that Sunday morning Dr. Francis Donlon called me. He said, "I have your dear brother here in St. Anthony's emergency room, Ann." Then he added, "But he is all right. I'll put him on."

Father D said, "Ann, I don't want to get anyone excited. I just want you to know I'm here. Will you tell Agnes and Kay?"

I assured him that I would, and that we would be there with him very soon.

When we arrived at St. Anthony De Padua Hospital, Cardinal Cody was arriving too. He had been at the seminary in Mundelein, and on hearing of Michael's illness, had rushed back to Chicago.

Father D had been awake all night with the distress of chest pains, and he suspected that these were symptoms of a heart attack. Earlier that morning he had left home, debating with himself on the way if he should first speak at St. Ferdinand's Church as he had planned, or if he should go directly to the hospital to "check it out."

It was fortunate that he decided on the latter, and it was fortunate also that Dr. Donlon made a habit of being in the emergency room on Sunday mornings. It was also typical of my brother to drive himself to the hospital.

For the first three days Father D's condition was unchanged; we waited close by, taking our turns to visit him for three minutes out of every hour. Gradually, there was a change for the better.

Mike was very weak and he had the discomfort of the heart-monitoring machinery attached to him; but he was as pleasant as ever, and very appreciative of our concern for him. His illness had struck him so suddenly that all of his appointments and obligations were still foremost in his mind. When one of us would walk into his room she would jot down the messages that he would ask to be taken care of for him. It was unbelievable that he knew so many phone numbers from memory. The calls he asked us to make were mostly in regard to his campaign work, but some were to elderly friends whom he knew would be worried if they did not hear from him personally. He would say, "Just tell them that I'm all right."

When our brother was released from intensive care and transferred to a private room, we were overjoyed. His visitors were still limited to the cardinal, the Lourdes' priests, and Agnes, Kay, and me. However, it was impossible to keep his friends away from him. Numerous people, unannounced at the desk downstairs, dropped in just for a minute.

He was deluged with cards and notes, many of which came from people he had never met; but the personal messages from his parish children delighted him most.

As soon as he could leave his bed, Bishop Dempsey was out meeting other patients in the corridor.

Dr. Donlon recommended some weeks of recuperation away from the city, and Kay's home would be ideal. Even in the cold of January, the rustic country scene would be restful; and the slightly hilly land would be a good place to test his heart, as he walked the quiet roads with his nephews. Kay was most solicitous about his health and gave him excellent care.

But soon, though under doctor's orders to live at a much slower pace than had been his custom, Father D became anxious to return to Lourdes.

Of course he was well aware of the fact that his heart was damaged. He planned to continue to work with the campaign, but he would do less of the work himself during the coming year. However, we knew that once he was back in Lawndale there would be no stopping him.

On his return to Lourdes, the parishioners welcomed him with the warmth of one very large family; and Father Purtell and Father Jasinski, Dorothy and Virginia, all wanted to do everything they could to help him.

By May, we had a family wedding taking place in Lourdes. At this time Father D joined Jackie Dunn and Michael Brown in marriage.

During the reception which followed in the school hall, the loud music echoing through the open windows attracted a great number of neighborhood children. They lined the stairway and the window sills as they clapped their hands in time with the music. One of the teenagers brought his own musical instrument and joined in with the band. Michael was very happy to have "his kids" taking part in the celebration.

Then, there were outside activities in which Michael, as a bishop, was invited to participate. It was not only because his three sisters were Immaculata alumnae that he was the bishop who was asked to offer the Mass in Holy Name Cathedral on the Golden Anniversary of the high school; but also because, as a professor at Mundelein College for many years, he had become very well acquainted with the BVM Sisters.

I was especially impressed by the homily he had prepared for this occasion. The Women's Liberation Movement was prominent at the time, and he was speaking to hundreds of women of various ages. His topic was "The Role of the Catholic Woman in the World Today." Her career, as he saw it, was to bring the love of God to the world about her. He stressed that, "By nature, a woman has a sensitivity to the thoughts and the feelings of others. Taking time to listen, and letting others know that you really care about what happens to them, is sometimes the most important thing you can do," he said.

On my way home from the cathedral, I happened to pass the scene of an automobile accident. A woman was crying as she stood alone beside her damaged Cadillac. Instinctively, I parked my car and went back to sympathize with her and to ask if I could help in any way. As I stood with her for a few minutes, I realized that my brother was right — sometimes all we do have to offer is a little concern.

That summer we appreciated Father D more than ever because we could have lost him; but he was still with us. Surely he was equally happy.

It was at this time that Father Tom Purtell was transferred from Lourdes and was succeeded by Father Cyril Nemecek. Father Nemecek, having served on the Conference on Religion and Race, was already well-acquainted with the bishop.

Mike turned fifty-five in September of 1973, but he looked much older than his years. Although he sometimes appeared fatigued, his ever-present smile gave us an assurance that everything was fine.

Then, with the coming of autumn, his confirmation schedule, combined with the campaign business, kept him very busy.

Although Father Robert Monticello had been appointed associate general secretary of the United States Catholic Conference the previous December, he remained as acting director of the campaign during the period in which an intensive search for a successor was conducted.

In August of 1973, the appointment of Father Lawrence J. McNamara to this post was announced by Bishop James Rausch, general secretary for the USCC. Father McNamara was formerly executive director of Catholic Family and Community Services in the Kansas City -St. Joseph, Missouri, Diocese and pastor of an inner-city parish there. He was chosen from nearly forty persons whose names had been submitted for the campaign post. "The stated purpose of the campaign is to break the circle of poverty by helping people help themselves," Bishop Rausch commented. "Father McNamara is uniquely suited to this assignment." And indeed, Father McNamara's achievements in his local diocese were remarkable.

One of the first things Father McNamara wanted to do was to confer with Bishop Dempsey on the direction that he might see the campaign taking. However, there was such a flurry of activity between mid-September and the first week of October — when Father McNamara was scheduled to leave for the fall travel — that it didn't seem feasible to attempt a trip to Chicago. Anyway, a stop in Chicago was one of the fourteen scheduled for that particular fall. So Father McNamara decided to wait and take advantage of being in Chicago for the meetings with the press, clergy conferences, opportunities to be on radio and television, and all the other things that characterized the fall travel.

Father McNamara arrived in Chicago on Tuesday, October 16. He and Michael had lunch together on Wednesday. Much later Father McNamara told me: "It was truly an inspirational moment for me to finally meet in person the man about whom I had heard so much, both before coming to the national campaign and after joining the staff. He was good, humble, self-effacing, dedicated to giving everything within him and about him to the service of the poor and to helping bring closer the peace and justice of the Kingdom of Christ. We talked about the campaign in general, the clergy conference for Chicago priests, which I was to address that day, etc. He gave me some excellent suggestions for what might be the most effective way to approach the clergy conference — particularly stressing that I probably could address myself more to how to make the educational program for the campaign a reality in their parishes than to 'motivating them' about the campaign in general. If any group of priests in the country were already motivated, it was those of the Archdiocese of Chicago. The priests and people of Chicago were as committed to the campaign as any group in America.

"Bishop Dempsey's suggestion that we go to work very seriously on how to make *education* about poverty and justice both an event and an effective one for the ordinary Catholic person throughout the country, gave real insight into the depth and accuracy of his perception as to where the greatest single effort — the most difficult challenge facing the campaign — might lie. 'Education' sounds like such a simple term and such a relatively easy thing to do. Everyone is in favor of education. All you have to do is say the word, and people unanimously nod and say: 'Yes! That's what is needed . . .*education.*' But effectively educating is a lot more difficult to do than talking about how imperative the need for such might be. The bishop clearly perceived that and wanted to be sure that I did too. Bishop Dempsey, in a very gentle and fatherly way, wanted to be certain that I did not assume that simply producing books, booklets, curricular for schools, radio and television spots would be the answer. Important as such work was, a way would have to be found, both to make sure that whatever it was we produced somehow or other came to the attention of ordinary people. Taking a step further, having them emotionally and intellectually aware of poverty, injustice, and oppression might not really accomplish what we intended. There is a great deal of difference between someone asserting that it is a terrible thing for people to search endlessly for jobs that aren't there, work all their lives for nothing but the minimum wage, and end up with no pensions and perhaps bodies broken by the kind of work they had to do, etc.

"Just knowing these kinds of things and agreeing that they shouldn't be, might not change anything. What Bishop Dempsey was suggesting was that I talk with the priests about how we informed people in such a way that they *moved with urgency* toward the kind of changes demanded by justice and compassion. We are still searching and groping for more effective ways to do that. It has been a preoccupation of those who work in the Educational Component — and in the last year or so has been a very clearly-shared concern of those who work in the Grant Program. This search for ways to change the hearts of people as well as affect their minds has more or less been a preoccupation of all of my visits during the fall travel of 1974, 1975, and 1976. In close to one hundred dioceses I have shared the luncheon conversation of October 17, 1973, with thousands of people: laity, religious, clergy, bishops."

Among the Educational Component's core themes for 1973 were: Christianity as a Lifestyle; where poverty of spirit, accepted dependence on God, and other men, lead to a community of sharing trust; and self-realization through the common good.

In order for Michael to lessen his duties as he planned at the time of his hospitalization, it was necessary to find a bishop in each of twelve episcopal regions throughout the country to assume responsibility and be the spokesman in his own locality. No one person ever again took the position of national director of the Campaign for Human Development. So, in effect, Bishop Dempsey was replaced by twelve bishops when the structure was changed.

And, in an effort to help Michael on the Chicago scene, Cardinal Cody appointed Father James Moriarity to the local campaign post. Father Moriarity, having just finished working on another program, the State Aid Campaign, was assigned to the Chancery. He said, "I went with Bishop Dempsey and sat by his side watching him allocating proposals and funding them."

Michael continued to work with his neighborhood group who studied the proposals. Father Moriarity would meet with him in the rectory office at Lourdes. He sensed that it was difficult for Michael to climb the stairs and that therefore the bishop spent most of his day in his office. The new campaign priest found it amusing that the children passing the rectory would come to the window to wave to them.

The 1973 collection was another manifestation of the charity in the hearts of the Catholics of our country.

CHAPTER TWENTY

THE TIME FOR FOND FAREWELL

ON A SATURDAY morning, early in January, 1974, Kay called to tell me that Father Ray Jasinski and Sister Joanne had taken Michael into St. Anthony's Hospital. Our brother was suffering from indigestion, and the doctor wished to take the precaution of hospitalizing him. The indigestion proved to be a re-occurrence of his heart problem.

By Monday, Michael readily agreed to accept a pacemaker, which was expected to be very helpful in his situation. In the afternoon he was in good spirits, telling us how the pacemaker would operate. Agnes, Kay, and I left him at dinner time, hopeful that he was doing well.

An hour later, a hospital spokesman phoned, summoning us back to St. Anthony's. Father D's heart had stopped, and then started again.

Dr. Donlon told us that he had explained this to Michael by saying, "Bishop, St. Peter took you right up to the gates and then brought you back." Then the doctor added, "You can talk to him like that."

Seeing Father D in the intensive care unit's machinery and with the oxygen equipment attached to him, would easily have broken the spirits of those who loved him so much; but, through his obvious great discomfort, he could still smile and welcome us. This was our consolation.

Since we always had been a very close family, it wasn't surprising that about thirty members of our clan were gathered in St. Anthony's that evening. When Father Phil Cahill arrived, I said "Father, I knew you'd be here. You have been with us on all our happy and sad occasions through the years."

Bishop Abramowicz also remained in the hospital until late that night. St. Anthony's personnel extended the same hospitality to us as they had given to our brother.

The nurse assigned to Michael requested permission to stay on for another shift, saying, "The bishop is used to me now."

During the long night she would come out to speak to us in the waiting room. At one time she said, "He is just a beautiful person. Instead of being concerned about himself, he is telling me that I should get some rest."

At six-thirty in the morning of January 8, when the first signs of dawn were beginning to appear, his last moments were near. In his death, just as in his life, he was an inspiration to those who had the privilege of observing his complete acceptance of God's will.

As we, his sisters, stood close to him, he held our hands. The family, as well as the hospital Sisters who had become attached to him during his two short confinements in the intensive care unit, crowded together in the small room.

Then, as the elderly chaplain of St. Anthony's quietly read the prayers for the dying, Bishop Dempsey spoke the words that so fittingly closed his lifetime in this world.

"I thank the Lord that I have been able to give my life to the services of His poor. This has been my greatest joy." Then he added, "I thank the Lord for giving me this extra year to get things in order. Thank you girls for all you've done."

Kay said tearfully, "Mike, you'll be with all of our loved ones."

He smiled and said, "Yes."

I added, "Give them our love."

He said, "Oh, I will."

Then I continued, "Father D, always stay close to us and keep praying for us."

Again he said so pleasantly, "Oh, I will."

We knew then that we would have our own special intercessor in Heaven.

Michael was alert until his last breath. When he closed his eyes we quietly prayed a rosary. Then, as the group of us reluctantly turned about to leave, a nursing Sister, wiping her tears, said, "I have been at the deathbed of a saint."

Kay's daughter, Mary Satera, a nurse, had been observing the heart monitor. She said that she had never before witnessed a person's speaking so coherently when all of his life signs had ceased.

Just minutes after Michael's death, Bishop Abramowicz, who had returned to the hospital very early in the morning, began a Mass for his dear friend, and we all attended in the hospital chapel.

Cardinal Cody phoned then and spoke to Kay and Agnes and me individually. He was very grieved by the loss of his devoted auxiliary; and he graciously invited the family to meet with him and a few priests in the dining room of Holy Name Cathedral to make arrangements for the funeral. We were treated as honored guests. The services began on Wednesday morning with the cardinal celebrating a Mass at Our Lady of Lourdes for all of the school children.

Throughout the day, and until the following afternoon, Michael, dressed in his beautiful white vestments, lay in state beneath the altar of the church he loved. If a person who had never heard of Bishop Dempsey had sat there in a pew, he could have learned precisely the kind of man this was, just from observing his wake.

As numerous people braved the inclement weather to pay their respects to the bishop it was apparent that many felt a very personal loss. I especially remember the parish janitor being overcome with sorrow.

Teenagers wanted to talk to us and to tell us that they were his very close friends. They told us of instances in which the bishop had done something special for them. One broken-hearted boy was Juan, a boy who was alone in the world until the bishop became his legal guardian and put him into a Catholic boarding school.

But the little children who waited in line for their turn to hold the bishop's hand truly described him more eloquently in their silent tributes than any words could have accomplished. Some were too small to reach over the casket, so they lifted their weight on to the satin-covered side of it in order to stroke his face or to briefly hold his hand. Though the lining of the casket was being detached, no one would think of denying his little friends their fond farewells. And, what would delight the bishop more than to have his face, his hands, and his vestments completely covered with the fingerprints of his beloved children?

The Knights of St. Peter Claver, dressed in their fine uniforms, lined the aisle of Lourdes as another Mass for the bishop began that evening. The members of the Ladies' Auxiliary, all clad in white, attended in large numbers. As all of our Chicago bishops concelebrated this Mass for their fellow bishop, Lourdes' choir and combo rendered the heartfelt music which typified the black community.

The entire family had remained all that day at Lourdes, and the generosity of the parish people was unforgettable. Apparently many had cancelled all of their activities as they would have done at the time of a death in their own families. The ladies brought such quantities of home-cooked food that everyone who stopped in at the rectory was welcome to have something to eat.

On Thursday, our dear Father D's remains were transported to Holy Name Cathedral, where he would lie in state until the funeral on the following day.

The Knights of St. Peter Claver and the Knights of Columbus kept a constant vigil at his side, as hundreds of people, brushing the heavy snow from their clothing, walked in to view the man who was called "the friend of the poor."

The prayer of St. Francis of Assisi might have provided the theme of Bishop Michael Dempsey's life:

> *"Lord, make me an instrument of Thy peace;*
> *where there is hatred, let me sow love;*
> *where there is injury, pardon;*
> *where there is doubt, faith;*
> *where there is despair, hope;*
> *where there is darkness, light;*
> *and where there is sadness, joy.*
>
> *"O Divine Master, grant that I may not so much*
> *seek to be consoled as to console;*
> *to be understood as to understand;*
> *to be loved, as to love;*
> *for it is in giving that we receive,*
> *it is in pardoning that we are pardoned,*
> *and it is in dying that we are born to eternal life."*

A wake service was conducted at the cathedral that evening. Bishop Thomas Grady presided at this Liturgy. It was a very moving service. Bishop Grady had a very difficult time in giving the homily. He was so filled with emotion that he had to stop once or twice to regain the composure needed to go on. The third time his voice broke, he simply gave up trying to complete what he wanted to say and went back to his chair.

Then Friday came, and the cathedral was filled to capacity for the funeral. The processional was truly reminiscent of the happy day of our brother's consecration. As the pageant of hierarchy and clergy of every denomination, wearing dignified clerical vestments, ascended the long aisle and slowly took their designated places within the vast sanctuary, one could envision Bishop Dempsey's tireless efforts in ecumenism encircling the throng of people.

Father McNamara described the Mass of the Resurrection as a "hope-filled, love-filled, and joy-filled moment." He said, "I, and most of those around me, unashamedly gave up trying to hold back tears of inspiration, gratitude, and joy. It was not so much sadness in the face of death and separation as it was the celebration of a life that had been truly lived in the footsteps of the Master — the joy of knowing that Christ had lived among us in the person of this beautiful man who had now finished the course, faithful to the end, and was at last in the Kingdom of the Father. I will never forget that moment in which the sun suddenly came through the great window of Holy Name Cathedral and seemed to shine directly on the bishop."

The solemn ritual of the Mass was concelebrated by our own cardinal and bishops, and their love for their brother bishop was evidenced by their tears.

Anyone who might have cast his eyes about in the magnificent cathedral could have observed the kinds of people who were Mike's friends. They were the old and the young; the unknown and the eminent; the poor and the affluent; the well and those who walked with great effort; the people of every race and every faith — these were his friends.

The celebration of the Mass proceeded with indescribable splendor. The traditional organ and violin music and the singing which customarily was echoed from the choir loft high above the elegant entrance-way, now alternated with the Lourdes' combo and choir resounding from a prominent place within the sanctuary. Mike might well have been bursting with pride, for surely he would have wanted everyone to hear "his kids."

The drums of the combo rumbled as the children sang the old black Baptist hymn, "Precious Lord, Take My Hand."

It was evident to all that the Lord had long ago taken Michael Dempsey's hand and led him into a lifetime of service to his fellow-men. Now the precious Lord had taken him home.

The service in St. Joseph's Cemetery in River Grove, was held in the beautiful chapel which Mike, himself, had dedicated only seven months before. Then he was laid to rest beside his parents and his brother-in-law, Bill Hastings.

The tribute of the Tri-Faith staff gave a message of hope that surely would please our bishop: "His loss will leave a great vacuum among the ranks of the fighters for justice. But his dream has become our dream as we go forward, committed to the unfinished task of eradicating injustice and poverty."

And three years later, Father McNamara said: "I have attempted to make the Campaign for Human Development follow the example of Bishop Michael Dempsey. Those working on the national level and the great preponderance of diocesan directors and the people who surround them, have attempted to live lives both as individuals and as a movement which would reflect the simplicity — in the highest meaning of that word — which characterized his whole life. We have tried to use less and less for ourselves so that there would be more and more to share with the poor. I think Bishop Dempsey would like that. I think he felt deeply that the goods of this world were entrusted to all of God's children in stewardship and that this stewardship needed to begin in our own individual and personal lives. I believe that he felt that the justice of Christ called for us not so much to give out of our abundance while retaining an abundance for ourselves but rather of sharing what we have — including our very lives — with those for whom these gifts, in the Will of God, were truly intended. In the spirit of the bishop, there has been a national effort to make the Campaign for Human Development be much more than the raising of money so that projects could be funded and educational materials produced. Thousands of people have attempted to make it a re-evaluation of our priorities as individuals, as families, as a people, so that justice, which must be there before compassion and charity are authentic, may some day prevail. Finally, we have attempted to not only make funds available so that groups of poor or oppressed people could have a new day and a new life, but also to find ways to bring poor and non-poor together so that each could share the suffering, the hopes, and the joys of the other, somewhat as Bishop Dempsey shared with his people all that was his life and theirs in the parishes where he ministered.

"The Campaign for Human Development, the people of the parishes in which he served, the poor of Chicago and of America, the priests of Chicago, and the bishops of our country owe a great debt of gratitude to him. He was the kind of man, priest and bishop who could affect our lives profoundly. Our Holy Father, Pope Paul VI, has said on more than one occasion that the people of this age are less inclined to learn from teachers than from witnesses, and that if they do learn from a teacher it is because that person is also a witness. Bishop Dempsey was a witness. I believe it is for that reason more than any other that he was also one of the great teachers of his time."

As a testimony to the value of the campaign to which Michael gave every ounce of his energies, a study conducted by the management firm of Booz, Allen, and Hamilton, in 1976, concluded that the projects funded by the Campaign for Human Development had generally made good progress toward the achievement of both campaign and project goals.

The report stated that approximately one-third of the projects resulted in spin-off efforts, with other groups creating similar projects and that campaign funds assisted almost half the projects to attract additional funding from other sources.

In 1976, the collection was again up to eight and a half million dollars.

Great things have happened because of the campaign: depressed people have been able to organize and thereby rise to a position wherein they can speak for themselves; ethnic groups, senior citizens, communities of people who have suffered because of adverse conditions, and people who have been excluded from gainful employment, are among the thousands who are now experiencing a new day and a new life — and the Campaign for Human Development still continues — because people do care about their fellow-men.

In closing, I wish to express my gratitude to God for gracing my life with the close association of a brother who was His humble servant and the servant of His people. My life and the lives of all of our family have been greatly enriched by Mike's presence.

ADDENDA

Excerpt from *Journal — City Council — Chicago*, January 16, 1974:

"TRIBUTE PAID TO LATE MOST. REV. MICHAEL R. DEMPSEY, AUXILIARY BISHOP AND VICAR GENERAL OF CHICAGO ARCHDIOCESE.

Honorable Richard J. Daley, Mayor, on behalf of himself and the other members of the City Council presented the following proposed resolution:

WHEREAS, Almighty God in His Infinite Wisdom has called to his eternal reward on January 9, 1974, The Most Reverend Michael R. Dempsey, Auxiliary Bishop and a Vicar General of the Chicago Archdiocese; and

WHEREAS, Bishop Dempsey was ordained in 1943. From 1944 until 1961 he served at St. Mary of the Lake Parish on the North side of Chicago. From 1962 to 1964 he was an Associate Pastor at St. Francis De Paula Parish on the South side of Chicago. Since 1965 he had been Pastor of Our Lady of Lourdes Parish. He was one of five Auxiliary Bishops of the Chicago Archdiocese and served as coordinator of the Church's inner city apostolate. His untimely death came as a result of a heart ailment that first struck him in November, 1972, and

WHEREAS, Bishop Dempsey headed the very successful "Campaign For Human Development" a national once-yearly collection for self-help money for the poor, from its beginning in 1970 until last year. He was a board member of the Chicago Conference on Religion and Race as well as the former Interreligious Council on Urban Affairs. He founded "Lawndale For Better Jobs" after his assignment to Our Lady of Lourdes, which later became "Tri-Faith Employment Agency" a major project of the conference on Religion and Race; and

WHEREAS, Bishop Dempsey was a gentle man who worked hard in a largely behind the scenes effort in behalf of poor people, a man whose one goal was to struggle that the rights of all men be recognized, especially of the oppressed, of minorities. He was a man of peace and prayer. His place will not be filled in the church in Chicago and in the United States; now, therefore,

Be It Resolved, That the Mayor and members of the City Council of the City of Chicago, in meeting assembled this 16th day of January, A.D., 1974, publicly express their sorrow at the untimely passing of Bishop Michael R. Dempsey, devoted servant of God and champion of the poor, and further express their deep sympathy to the family of Bishop Michael R. Dempsey; and

Be It Further Resolved, That a suitable copy of this resolution be presented to the family of Bishop Michael R. Dempsey.

Alderman Bilandic moved to *Suspend the Rules Temporarily* to permit immediate consideration of and action upon the foregoing proposed resolution. The motion *Prevailed*.

On motion of Alderman Bilandic (seconded by Alderman Rhodes) the foregoing proposed resolution was *Adopted*, unanimously, by a rising vote."

OFFICE OF THE MAYOR

CITY OF CHICAGO

RICHARD J. DALEY
MAYOR

September 30, 1970

Most Reverend Sir:

As you know, we in Chicago who are working with public and private
agencies have been deeply concerned with the problem of poverty among
the uneducated, the unskilled, the young and the aged. These are
national problems as well. The most critical resource of the United
States is its people -- and better ways must be found to conserve and
develop that resource.

I am asking you to serve on a Citizens' Committee (the Chicago Committee on Urban Opportunity) as a representative from the Archdiocese of
Chicago. In this capacity you will be representing an agency which
has long worked for the development of Chicago and its people. I am
hopeful that you will be able to accept this appointment, as it is
only with the participation and involvement of citizens like yourself
that we can achieve the objectives of the Economic Opportunity Act,
giving every individual an opportunity to work and live in decency
and dignity.

With kindest personal regards,

Respectfully yours,

Mayor

The Most Reverend Michael R. Dempsey
Auxiliary Bishop of the
    Archdiocese of Chicago
Our Lady of Lourdes Church
1444 South Keeler Avenue
Chicago, Illinois 60623

ARCHDIOCESE OF CHICAGO
POST OFFICE BOX 1979
CHICAGO, ILLINOIS 60690

Office of the Coordinator
for the Inner City Apostolate

May 8, 1968

FOR RELEASE: STATEMENT OF BISHOP-ELECT MICHAEL R. DEMPSEY

I AM GRATEFUL TO OUR HOLY FATHER, POPE PAUL VI FOR THE CONFIDENCE HE HAS PLACED IN ME, BY SELECTING ME AS AUXILIARY BISHOP OF CHICAGO.

THE PRIESTS, SISTERS, AND LAY PEOPLE OF THE INNER CITY AND OF VICARIATE IV HAVE BEEN SUCH A HELP AND INSPIRATION FOR ME. I HOPE THAT I SHALL BE ABLE TO SERVE THEM MORE COMPLETELY WITH THE FULLNESS OF THE PRIESTHOOD WHICH SHALL SOON BE MINE.

QUITE AWARE OF MY GREAT UNWORTHINESS TO SHARE THE RESPONSIBILITY OF THE EPISCOPATE, I SHALL RELY AS ALWAYS UPON THE LOYALTY AND ENTHUSIASM OF THE PRIESTS, SISTERS AND LAITY OF CHICAGO WHOSE COOPERATION I TREASURE SO MUCH.

GRATEFUL FOR THE DEEP FRIENDSHIPS WHICH I SHARE WITH SO MANY RELIGIOUS LEADERS OF OTHER COMMUNIONS AND SYNAGOGUES, I KNOW THAT THEY TOO SHARE MY JOY IN ATTAINING THE EPISCOPACY.

I AM HONORED TO SERVE AS THE AUXILIARY BISHOP OF ONE OF THE GREATEST CHURCHMEN OF OUR TIMES, JOHN CARDINAL CODY, WHOSE CLOSE FRIENDSHIP AND PRIESTLY INSPIRATION I CONSIDER TO BE ONE OF THE GREATEST JOYS OF MY TWENTY-FIVE YEARS IN THE PRIESTHOOD.

IN THE CHURCH OF JESUS CHRIST, THE BISHOP IS CALLED "SERVANT" OF GOD'S HOLY PEOPLE. I TRUST THAT I SHALL BE ABLE TO SERVE MORE FULLY THE WHOLE CHURCH OF CHICAGO, ESPECIALLY MY DEAR FRIENDS IN THE INNER CITY AND GOD'S BELOVED POOR, IN WHOSE MIDST I AM PRIVILEGED TO DWELL.

MICHAEL RYAN DEMPSEY